Dark Exodus

To Kimberly

Thank you for

supporting the
Last Girls

Beverly Parkhurst
Moss

Dark Exodus

Lost Girls of Sudan

Beverly Parkhurst Moss

Acknowledgments

It would be impossible to acknowledge all of the people who have brought their influence and knowledge forward to help make *Dark Exodus* a reality.

First there is Stephanie Montgomery, who insisted I attend the Steel Magnolia's small event one evening at the Fellowship Church. I almost didn't go. "Oh come on," she insisted. "They're serving desserts. You'll love it." Who could resist that?

I went, and to my amazement, met Anne Worth. It was her speech about the Lost Girls that started this project.

Meanwhile, Stephanie threw herself wholeheartedly into this new venture by arranging for me to speak at a group function for women who appreciate wine.

From that first week, Anne Worth paved the way for each interview. She ran interference, stood by my side during a difficult business crisis, and arranged luncheons and readings for the book. She has become my comrade in arms. I can honestly say I could not have completed this project without her.

Then there is Neil Hoey, a talented illustrator and writer, gifted with incredible intuition. When I described my vision of the footprint in the desert sand, he reproduced it exactly the way

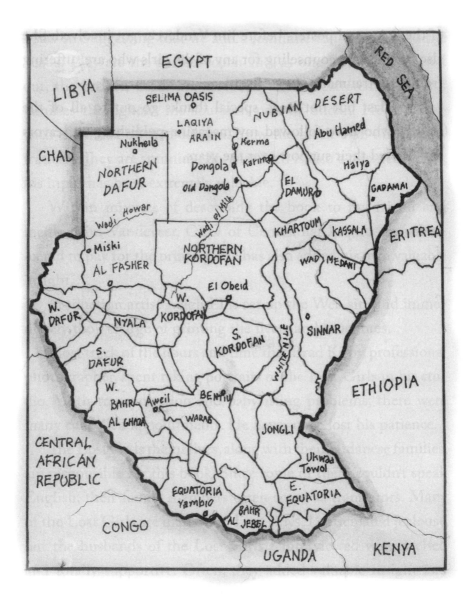

Sudan

A Brief History of Sudan

In ancient times, Sudan was known as the region of Nubia. With 918,000 square miles, it is the largest country in Africa. Starting at the Egyptian border, the Nile River flows to the southern border of Uganda. That vast area encompasses the scorching Sahara desert terrain of the North to swamps and rain forests in the South. Lost Boy John Bul Dau, co-author of "God Grew Tired of Us," describes the southern part of Sudan as a "land of milk and honey."

Sudan was originally Egyptian territory, between 1825 and 1880. Khartoum, first established as a military outpost in 1821, is located at the convergence of the Blue and White Nile Rivers. It is said that its name is derived from the spit of land at the convergence of the rivers, which resembles an elephant's trunk (khurtum). Over the years, Khartoum grew dramatically in prosperity because of the slave trade. In 1834, Khartoum became the capital of Sudan. Many European explorers used it as a base for their African expeditions.

In the late 1800s, Muhammad Ahmad, a Muslim religious leader believed to be a Mahdi, incited a revolt against the Egyptian government. He accused them of being puppets of the British, which, in his eyes, put them in the same category as infidels.

Like the Christian religion, Islam has its "end of time," and its "Day of Judgment." Muslims believe that when this happens, the Koran and its morality will be universally accepted. Similar to the book of Revelation in the Christian Bible, this Day of Judgment will be preceded by a period of great decline with terrible disasters, wars, and unimaginable suffering.

It is during this period that Muslims believe Allah will use a servant of superior morality, known as the Mahdi (a guide to the truth), who will steer humanity back to the right path.

This revolt eventually became a full-scale war as Ahmad strove to gain control of the Egyptian-ruled territory in Sudan.

Because of its strategic importance for trade routes to India, Sudan captured Britain's interest. The British soldiers, led by leaders who were known throughout the world as masters in strategy, were well trained and highly disciplined. Despite their military superiority, they were disconcerted when they found themselves faced with an enemy, sometimes armed only with spears and shields, who fought with such ferocity. The Mahdists, in their zealous pursuit of Jihad, or holy war, fought to the death. Even when they were mortally injured, they would lash out at their enemy until their dying breath.

Finally the British were able to win the day. Britain conquered the territory in 1898. British soldiers returned to England with tales about the fanatical Mahdists, who they referred to as dervishes.

In January 1899, an Anglo-Egyptian agreement was reached, giving Egypt control once again, but only in conjunction with the British.

Until 1955, Britain governed the territory as they industrialized the North, leaving the southern part of Sudan untouched, inhabited by tribes who valued cattle and farming. It was during this time that many European missionaries introduced Christianity to tribes in the southern region.

The people of Southern Sudan are often slender and tall with high cheekbones, noble profiles, graceful carriages, and ebony-colored skin. Characteristically they are intelligent, generous, and maintain strong family ties. The roles of the Sudanese people were clearly defined before the war. The women took care of the home, the children, and the village crops, while the men's lives revolved around their herds of cattle and goats, which they valued immensely. Even today, it is not unusual for a newborn child to be given two names, one that is Christian, and the other one relating to an animal.

The northern part of Sudan has a population that is predominantly Arab Muslim. Many of the people of this area are nomadic Arab tribesmen.

In the latter part of the 1900s, military regimes that favored Islamic-oriented governments began dominating national politics. The end result was two prolonged civil wars.

The first civil war ended in 1972. In the early '80s, an austerity program was imposed on Sudan to satisfy the International Monetary Fund (IMF) loan requirements and reduce a huge is used generally to describe armed gunmen who destroy their villages and kill many of their people. Another interpretation for the word is "horde."

The Janjaweed, whose forces contain a large number of career criminals and mercenaries, have become notorious for racist rhetoric, massacre, rape, and forced displacement. Although they are a separate entity, they cooperate and operate hand in hand with the government's military.

In recent years, the government has built a pipeline to transport the oil north to the Red Sea. Both China and Russia have no qualms when it comes to forging relationships with "pariah" dictatorships, so quickly China became Sudan's biggest customer. When the government realized there were vast reserves of oil in Sudan, they were more than willing to forge a relationship with Sudan despite the genocide against the people in the South. Along with China's growth in prosperity in recent years, more and more people are buying cars. 70 percent of China's oil comes from Sudan. Because China and Russia occupy permanent seats on the United Nations Security Council, they have used their positions to protect the government.

Many of the fleeing Sudanese first fled to Ethiopia, the closest country that promised refuge.

In 1991, when the regime of Mengistu Haile Mariam was overthrown in Ethiopia—forcing Mengistu into exile—the refugee camps came under attack. A fierce battle ensued between soldiers from the SPLA (Sudan's rebel army) and the Ethiopian military. Innocent civilians were caught in the crossfire, and the

Sudanese refugees were driven out. Desperate to escape, they were forced to cross the Gilo River, referred to by the Sudanese as the "big river," which forms a natural border between Ethiopia and Sudan. The Gilo River, running brown and fast, has strong currents, and in the spring, during the monsoon season, can become as wide as the Potomac River in Washington. At its strongest, uprooted trees, rocks, dead animals, and assorted debris are swept along making it extremely dangerous to cross. On the banks, crocodiles—some as large as full-grown men—wait for prey.

The Nile crocodile is one of the few species in the world known to attack people. They live in large communities, uniting, if necessary, to take down a much larger animal. One little known fact is that the Nile crocodile has been known to rise up on its rear legs and gallop up to thirty miles an hour on land.

Benjamin Ajak, a Lost Boy who is one of the authors of the book *They Poured Fire on Us from the Sky*, portrays one scene in heartbreaking detail as he paints a horrific picture of that terrible event. He describes bullets hissing among the fleeing refugees on the far banks as thousands of people rushed into the water and disappeared. He goes on to say that those who did manage to swim across did not dare to run up on the opposite bank because of gunfire.

Instead, they were forced to hide in the reeds among the crocodiles and deal with the horror of being attacked by those dangerous animals which were awakened by the scent of blood in the water. He even describes a scene where one woman was able to walk across the river, stepping on the backs of bodies that had *the word "genocide" in the 20th Century, defining it as: "Acts committed with intent to destroy, in whole or in part, a national, ethnic, racial, or religious group."*

Adopted in 1948 by the UN General Assembly, the definition has lasted for nearly six decades. The word refers to the mass murdering of defenseless civilians including men, women, and children.

In 1999, approximately four thousand Lost Boys and eighty-nine Lost Girls were brought from refugee camps in Africa and resettled in the United States. In recent years the Lost Boys have received a growing amount of national attention. However, the Lost Girls have gone relatively unnoticed.

Why did nearly four thousand Sudanese boys make it to America in 1999 as opposed to only eighty-nine girls? More of the boys survived because they were out in the country herding cattle and sheep when the attacks occurred in their villages. When they heard the gunshots and screams, they fled. The girls, along with their mothers and smaller children, were in their homes. Most of the adult men were killed. The women and girls were enslaved, brutally raped, or, as the Sudanese say, "used up." Those that did survive, hid in the jungle and began their long and dangerous trek to the camps.

In the Dinka tribe, women are highly valued and often serve as a measure of a man's wealth. A man who is wealthy often has multiple wives. When a child is born, as soon as he or she is old enough, the child sleeps in a sleeping hut with other children. Thus the families are large and extended. The Dinka people adore their children.

The girls who survived the dangerous journey were absorbed into existing families once they reached the refugee camps. The polite term is "fostered," but in many cases they became unpaid servants or were sold off to older men who paid a bride price of between five and fifty cows, which amounted to fortunes for people in the camp. Because of this, often the foster parents were reluctant to release the girls and allow them to go their own way because they were afraid of losing the bride price.

Once the girls were absorbed into families, they had little or no visibility. The boys, living together in groups, were highly visible. The UN, nervous that these groups of boys were ripe for recruitment into the SPLA, made arrangements to move them to Europe, Canada, Australia, and the United States.

Many of the Sudanese people I interviewed are skeptical about the survival of the peace accord. If it stays in place, some will return because they have a desperate desire to contribute to the welfare of their native country. Others simply do not want to take the risk.

Preface

Each one of the following sixteen interviews began the same. After the greeting, "Hello, how are you? Are you well?" I was offered a soft drink and water, served on a tray. I could not help but be impressed by the impeccable manners of the Lost Girls, a group of amazing women I was interviewing for the book *Dark Exodus*.

Each home I visited had shoes lined up by the door. Lavishly embroidered doilies covered the surfaces of sofas and chairs. Without exception, even though many of these homes and apartments were not in the best of neighborhoods, the homes were immaculate.

Then, as I cautiously broached the subject of each woman's amazing journey through the wilderness, it was as if I had run into an invisible brick wall.

The expression on my subject's face, originally bright and animated, became blank. As she stared off into the distance, her answers were brief. "The Arabs attacked my village. I had to run away. I was in the refugee camp, and then I came to America."

At first I was startled. Then awareness dawned. These women

Chapter One

Monica Warabek

what you do when you are seven years old. I ran into the jungle.

Villages in many parts of Sudan are arranged in a circular area that is usually surrounded by a fence. Unlike American houses, which contain several rooms under one roof, the family units in a Sudanese village are housed in multiple huts positioned in a semi-circle. They include a hut for the boys, another hut for girls, a hut for the mother, a hut for the father, and a visitor's hut.

No one could take the babies when they ran away. You had to choose. Stay with the babies and die, or leave them. Babies cry and the Arabs follow the sound. Everyone loves babies. It was very sad.

Hours later, my older brother, who had my two-year-old brother with him, found me. "Where is Mama and Poppa?" I asked him. At first he wouldn't answer. Finally, he said he didn't know where my mother was. I learned later that the Arabs had killed my father and two of my brothers. My brother told me the Arabs kept some of the girls. They raped them. Some of them they used up. Some they took into slavery.

My baby brother was only two years old and he cried constantly, "Where is Mama? I want Mama."

"I don't know where Mama is," I told him repeatedly. I was crying too.

If you tried to hide in the grass the Arabs could see the grass moving and they would track you, so we hid in the water. It was cold. With only our faces showing, we stayed in the water for hours. I saw a snake swim past. Snakes get very big in Africa and this one was huge. When we finally got out I had leeches all over my legs and feet. My father had many cows so we were used to drinking milk, but now there wasn't any milk because the Arabs had killed all of the livestock. My older brother foraged for food. I kept trying to comfort my little brother. He cried constantly.

"Where is Momma?" he would say over and over. Totally exhausted, he would finally fall asleep, but not for long. We were so tired, but we could not sleep. The mosquitoes were a torment. And to make matters worse, we were naked and barefoot.

The days passed in a blur. Every day I worried about my mother. Was she dead? Would I ever see her again? Surely if she was alive she would come looking for us. We were hungry, bewildered, and sad. I worried about my little brother.

Finally, after three weeks, we found other people who had also been hiding. Most of them, like us, were children. We all joined together and began walking. Suddenly I heard airplanes overhead. They began strafing us with bullets. People in front of me and behind me fell down, bleeding. They died.

I was shocked at how quickly people can die. They can be talking one moment and then just be gone. It was then I decided there was no God. If there was, how could he let this happen?

I wanted to die too. This was too hard. I was too tired, too scared, and I missed my mother, my father, and my brothers.

Then I saw people dying at the side of the road. They would sit down because their feet were sore or because they were so tired. They would close their eyes and then just die. Crying babies sat in the dirt alongside their dead mothers. "No," I told myself. "Don't die. Live!" So I decided to keep on. If I died, my baby brother would die.

From that time on, we only walked at night. It was too dangerous to walk during the day because the Arabs could see us. My feet were covered with blisters, and soon they were so sore I could only limp. I would sit down and try to extract the thorns from my feet by using a thorn. My bloody feet were leaving tracks, another thing to worry about since the scent of blood is a lure for wild animals.

We carried whatever food and water we could find with us. I was very scared because you can't see in the dark and you don't know what you might step on or run into, but it was the only way. My brother and I took turns carrying our baby brother. He was getting thinner and thinner.

There were so many things to be afraid of, including lions and hyenas. If we saw a lion we all gathered together and stood perfectly still. We didn't move a muscle, not even an eyelash. If the lion waited two hours—we waited two hours.

There is a certain tree in Africa that is very big. It has a thick trunk and branches that almost reach to the ground. It's like an umbrella. If we saw one of those trees, it was tempting to rush to it for shelter. But we had to be careful because it drew other things as well—dangerous things—snakes, lions, hyenas, even soldiers. Every living thing is drawn to shelter. Lakes, streams, and large trees were mixed blessings. They brought relief and life but also predators.

In 1992, we reached the camp in Kenya after walking for one month. I was shocked. I had never seen so many people. I would learn that, like us, they had suffered very much. No one seemed surprised by our arrival because people were coming into the camp every day. The first thing my brother did when we arrived was contact the Red Cross to see if we could find our mother.

Days after we arrived we found her. We rushed into Mama's arms. At first, all we could do was cry. As she held us in her arms, she cried too. She told us she thought we had been killed. It was such a relief. Suddenly things seemed better because finally we were together.

Once a month, we were given a small amount of corn, beans, some oil, and salt. It had to last a long time. Many months we ran out of food days before we were scheduled to receive more. Those days we went hungry. We refer to those days as "the dark days." If you had money you could buy meat.

The Islamic radicals periodically interrupted delivery of supplies and food to the camp. They knew that prolonged hunger and malnutrition were the means of killing the older inhabitants along with the weak and the ill. This is referred to as "genocide by attrition."

We lived in one room in a hut with mud walls. The camp was always very dirty and usually very hot, except for the two months of winter. Then everyone is miserable because it's hard to stay warm. Nothing is green, and everything is covered in dust. There's dust in your mouth when you eat, and dust gets in your eyes, even at night. Life is very hard, and a lot of people just lose heart and die.

Kakuma is located in Kenya. Originally built to hold 5,000

When the hostesses served the food I couldn't eat it. It smelled bad to me. I just drank tea and sodas.

When we landed in London it was dark. I was amazed at the lights. I could not understand what they were.

Many hours later we arrived in Virginia. I lived in an apartment with a roommate who was also a refugee. I was terrified to ride on the school bus. Although everyone was very kind, it was all so strange. I felt like I was living in a dream. Then one day a friend rushed up to me. "Come, come look outside," she said, dragging me by the hand out of the school. It was snowing. I was amazed. It was so beautiful, so cold and clean. I loved it. Still, I rarely talked because I was worried about my English, and I cried a lot. My body was in America, but my heart and soul were in Africa. My home in Africa is so very beautiful. I miss my mother, and I dream about her almost every night.

After she got out of school, Monica went to work in a hospital where she met her husband John, who is a Lost Boy. They came to Dallas in 2001. Monica's little brother is grown now. He is fully recovered and lives in Virginia. With great pride, Monica told me that he is very tall. The older brother who saved her went back to Sudan and was killed in the war. Monica's mother, who is still in the refugee camp in Kenya, has not only lost her husband, she has lost four sons.

At the end of the interview, Monica told me she had just talked to her mother a few days earlier and learned that a cousin was shot and killed while walking to the latrine during the night. Her mother told her that Kenya is worse than ever. As we talked, I could see the tears well up in Monica's eyes. "What can I do?" she told me she had asked her mother in frustration.

"I can't help her," she told me sadly. "Sometimes I don't know who I am. Am I African? Am I American?"

"You are an American," I replied, "and a brave one at that."

"How on earth had this young woman survived?" I wondered as I drove home from the interview. The image of a little girl walking through the jungle—naked and barefoot, with her two-year-old brother on her hip trying to comfort him as he cried, when she could be killed at any minute—was almost more then I could bear. Then I remembered Monica's parting words.

"God will lead the way," she said. "All we have to do is follow."

Recently I ran into Monica, and she told me that her mother had lost her sight in one eye.

"Has she been able to go to a doctor?" I asked.

"Yes, he gave her some medicine. But she needs an operation and it will cost $450 American dollars."

For the average American, $450 is not an enormous sum. But I'd come to realize that in a refugee camp, it can mean the difference between life and death.

"Is it cataracts?" I asked.

"Yes. She is nearly blind."

Author's Note:

Monica was forced to learn at a very young age that losing someone you love is a harsh and cruel reality. She has seen far too much death. Sometimes, when those memories come back to haunt her she wonders, "Did God forget about the Dinka people?" Yet, her faith sustains her.

Monica still has nightmares. Yet, she has adapted well and loves America and the American people. When we met recently at a luncheon, she told me with great pride that she and her husband had just become American citizens. What she wants more than anything is an education and to be able to help her mother get out of the refugee camp. When I asked her what field she would choose if she had an education, she replied it would be either in nursing or childcare. She has always loved children.

Chapter Two

Margaret Kuol

My God, you are the strong God, You care about your people all of the time. We have been running. The country of Sudan has been destroyed. We hear the bombs and guns all of the time, while we are running and running. God, your people are being eaten by lions and hyenas. When we run to the river, the crocodiles are waiting. So who will wipe our tears? It is You alone. No one, nobody else. You are the only one who can wipe our tears.

Margaret Kuol's Story

Margaret and her family lived in the city of Bor, a thriving town on the shores of the Nile River. She remembers the excitement and optimism that was prevalent in her home while she was growing up. Bor was becoming modernized. Telephone lines were being put up, an electrical plant was being built, and the future looked bright. Her father, a doctor at the local hospital, was affluent and a respected member of the community. Because her parents were part of the Dinka tribe, Margaret had relatives who lived in villages throughout southern Sudan. She attended school wearing the government-required uniform for girls—leggings, a long dress, and white headscarf. Her teachers and some of her playmates were Muslims. At twelve years of age, she was in every way a normal child.

When the second civil war in Sudan broke out in 1983, Bor was the first town to come under attack by the government and the dreaded Janjaweed.

Her story is as follows:

Some of my friends were Christian and some were Muslim. My life, up until the attack, was a happy one. Everyday I would hurry home from school, pull off the required headscarf and pants and rush outside to be with my friends. The Arab children would invite us to their homes and give us dates which were delicious. Some of the Muslim girls were our girlfriends. We would accompany them to their mosque and recite verses from the Koran. When my father found out about this one day, he became very upset. Sitting us down he gave us a stern lecture. "You are Christian, and the Muslim people are not good," he warned. He proceeded to tell us about the war that had occurred in the'50s. We listened politely, but his recollections of that war seemed very far away to me. "This is not anything that could ever happen again," I told myself. "My Muslim friends like me. They would never cause me harm."

The moment my father went back to work, we would run out to be with our playmates, and when they asked us to go with them to the mosque, we didn't hesitate.

Our Muslim friends also got into trouble when they visited our homes. On Sundays, they would go with us to church where they would learn about Jesus and the Bible. If their parents found out, they were beaten. But that didn't stop them. None of us cared about the color of our skin, and it didn't matter if we were Muslim or Christian. We were all just children who wanted to play together. To this day I can recite both the Koran and the Bible.

Another huge treat was the movies. We didn't have an indoor theater so a screen was set up outside, and we paid a penny to sit on the ground and watch. Many of the films were American Westerns or Arab movies. We enjoyed them immensely.

Then a strange thing began to occur. My Muslim friends and their families began to leave. We would see many of them on the boats moving slowly down the Nile. "Where are you going?" I would ask, when I saw them walking with their families towards the river.

The replies were often vague. "Oh we're just going on a holiday." Others would reply, "We're going to see relatives." I was bewildered. The town began to seem empty, and I missed my Muslim friends.

Then one morning I woke up early to hear dogs barking and birds screeching and cawing. I also heard what I thought were doors slamming. They were actually gunshots and bombs.

"Get the children and run," my mother yelled as she frantically threw some supplies and food together.

We didn't dare go to the river because of the crocodiles and snakes, so we ran into the woods. My entire family escaped. There we found other survivors. We lived for three months on fruit we found in the jungle. It was the monsoon season and it rained every day. The mosquitoes swarmed around us in clouds. It was impossible to sleep.

The heat and moisture around the Nile River creates the perfect environment for mosquitoes. More recently, the West Nile virus, a blood-borne disease also carried by mosquitoes, has spread throughout all of Africa.

My father, believing the worst was over, decided we should return to Bor. Some of the other survivors had already scattered to different villages. We returned, and even though we were nervous, we tried to settle back into our normal routine. My Muslim friends were gone and I no longer felt carefree. I realized the world was a dangerous place.

Then, early one morning Bor was attacked again. But this time, the Arabs went door to door, killing the occupants. We could hear the gunshots and the soldiers yelling, "Allahu Akbar," (God is the greatest) followed by the screams of people dying. We knew that if you tried to escape by car, the Arabs would stop the car, pull everyone out, and kill you on the spot. We ran behind the buildings. It was there I saw my friend. She was just sitting there quietly at the side of the alley, with her baby tied on her back.

"Get up," I pleaded. "Don't stop. You have to keep moving."

Other people gathered around her urging her to get up, warning her that if she didn't she would die.

"I'm too tired. I can't go on," she said over and over, while we begged her to come with us.

Finally we had to leave. Later that night I heard that others had passed by her body and the body of her child. Both bodies were mutilated. I am still haunted by this. I can't understand why she wouldn't come. She gave up hope. If you lose hope, you die.

The Arabs took over our town. Meanwhile we were running. We would find a village, the Arabs would track us, and two or three days later they would attack that village and we would run again.

It was during one of these raids that my brother and my father were murdered. The attack seemed to come out of nowhere, and we were all trying to escape. It was like a recurring nightmare, except there was no waking up because it was real. There would be the sudden rush of Arabs with fire in their eyes. Sometimes they would be on horseback or astride camels, other times they would be in jeeps and trucks. They would swoop down on our village, and then there would be the screams, sounds of gunshots, and the unnerving yells of "Allahu Akbar" as we fled for our lives.

It was during one of these times when we were fleeing the Arabs that I heard a shot directly behind me. When I turned I saw my father fall. I stood there staring in disbelief as his blood splashed onto the ground around his head. I turned and ran back. My brother and my father's bodies lay on the ground. My mother threw herself over my father's body. Then she stood up. "Run," she screamed as tears streamed down her face. "Run!"

We ran, and in so doing, became separated from each other. Like seeds, my family was scattered. Many of them were killed. Some I would never see again. As for my mother, it would be four years. I wouldn't see my sister Mary again until 2007.

Day after day I walked. Images of the devil-soldiers, hyenas, lions, snakes, fear of spider bites, hunger and unrelenting thirst—these were the things that occupied my mind. When I got too hungry and there was nothing to eat I chewed on grass and leaves. I got boils in my mouth and blisters on my face. The sun is so hot in the desert that it can fry you. I knew that I did not dare lie down because if I did, I would not get up again. I drank contaminated water without giving it a second thought. I sucked moisture out of mud and chewed on grass, and everyday I wondered, "Will I survive this day?" I knew I needed to keep up my spirits and not lose hope. I have always loved to sing so I made up a song and sang it endlessly.

The words are as follows:

"My God, you are the strong God

You care about your people all of the time.

We have been running. The country

of Sudan has been destroyed.

We hear the bombs and guns, all of the time

while we are running and running.

God, your people are being eaten by lions

and hyenas. When we run to the river, the

crocodiles are waiting.

So who will wipe away our tears?

It is you alone. No one, nobody else.

You are the only one who can wipe our tears."

Footsore and exhausted, Margaret finally arrived at the refugee camp in Ethiopia. It was an amazing and rare accomplishment for a teenage girl to survive such a horrendous journey. Often girls were kidnapped, killed, or raped along the way. While she was in the camp she met a young man who would become her husband. They returned to her ancestral village where he paid the required bride's price. Once they were married they returned to the camp. When the refugee camp in Ethiopia was attacked in 1991, Margaret was the mother of a two and a-half-year-old little girl and a six-month-old baby boy.

The camp was attacked and we were forced to run again. With thousands of people, all fleeing at once, I could not find my husband. To reach safety we had to cross the Gilo River, which divides Ethiopia from Sudan. The Gilo River is very dangerous. The water runs very fast, and it is infested with snakes and crocodiles. The men of the camp had quickly built a bridge made of rope. I had to take my children across that bridge, one at a time. I was very frightened. The first time I crossed the bridge, I clutched my baby boy tightly against my chest with one hand and used the other hand to hang onto the rope as I inched my way across. I handed him to a man on the other side and hurried back across the bridge. This time I got my little daughter, and, holding her by the hand, I led her across. Together with my children, I joined the other surviving refugees as we headed back to Sudan. Again, another long hard walk, but this time was even more difficult because I had children. After days of walking we arrived at Kakuma.

My daughter came down with Meningitis and almost died. Fortunately there were doctors in the camp and they were able to cure her. We were lucky. The years passed slowly. Because there was so little food we all looked like skeletons. Kakuma is truly a sea of human suffering. I prayed desperately for a way to give my children a better life. Then my name came up, and I had an opportunity to go to America. Almost at the same time, to my astonishment, I found my mother. She had been in another refugee camp all along. I debated whether or not I should go. "Go," she insisted. "Your children have no life here. Take them to America."

I arrived in Dallas and got a job at Six Flags. My first day was unnerving. I could speak very little English, but if I listened carefully I could understand what people were saying. I saw people get into this huge boat. It started to move, gained speed, and hit the water with a huge boom. Everyone screamed. I ran to my supervisor. "People are screaming!" I said in a loud whisper. She just looked at me. "How can she be so indifferent?" I wondered. "People are screaming!" I said, this time a little louder. It never occurred to me that people could scream because they are happy. I thought Six Flags was under attack.

I made friends with a missionary couple. They were wonderful. They insisted I get a car. We searched the classified ads in the newspaper and finally found a 1991 Dodge Shadow. The price was $900. I had $300 in the bank. They loaned me $600. I was working as much overtime as possible, and I tried to give them $100 out of my first paycheck.

"No Margaret, you need to feed your children," they replied. "Give yourself a few weeks."

I paid them $100 each month until the car was paid for. Learning to drive was a frightening thing. Shortly after getting the car I got into a wreck in the parking lot at Six Flags. I saw a car coming towards me and in trying to avoid it, I ran into another car.

The horrific events of September 11 affected Margaret deeply. The whole nation was in mourning. For Margaret, the attack brought back horrific memories and uncertainty about the future. She knew all too well what can happen in war. She remembers September 11th as if it happened yesterday.

One day, one of my co-workers came and grabbed my hand and pulled me into the break-room. Everyone had crowded around the television. When I saw the planes hitting the twin towers I began to cry. In Africa, when we are terribly frightened, our stomachs shake. So I immediately took off my blouse and tied it around my stomach. I sat down and began to pray.

"Oh God, did you save me from the war only to have it follow me here? Please save us God. You are a good God and these are good people. Do not let the terrorists destroy America like they have destroyed Sudan."

I drove home to my apartment. I was very afraid. Would the Arabs attack Texas next? There were many Sudanese people in my apartment. We all sat together and prayed. We asked God to save the United States, and we prayed for those people who had died in the Twin Towers.

Margaret and her husband were reunited when he was able to obtain a visitor's visa through a church program. Since then, he has returned to Africa to help rebuild Sudan. Margaret, who works as an interpreter, is the mother of six children. Her husband has never seen his youngest son. Margaret recently went to visit him. She is afraid to move back to Sudan, even though the peace accord is in place. She had a disturbing conversation with a cleaning lady while she stayed at a hotel in Yuba before returning to Texas.

There was an elderly Sudanese woman working for the hotel in housekeeping. We began talking and she told me how tired she was.

"Well mother, at least the country's at peace, and you do not have to be afraid," I said.

"Why do you think I am working, daughter? I have to feed

my children. Months ago there was a knock on our door late one night. These men took my husband away and I haven't seen him since. I am sure he is dead. The Arabs are not killing us openly now, but they are killing us in other ways."

Peace talks gained momentum in 2002 through 2004 with the signing of several accords. A final peace treaty of January 2005 granted the southern rebels autonomy for six years. When this period is over there are plans for a referendum that will address the issue of independence. Peace agreements between the Arabs and the rebels in the southern part of Sudan have been consistently violated by the Arabs since the '70s.

Margaret plans to stay in the United States. Her oldest daughter is in college and still drives the 1991 Dodge Shadow. She describes her thirteen-year-old daughter as a typical American teenager. Margaret and her sister Mary, who had fled to Egypt, were just reunited. They hadn't seen each other since 1983. Margaret has lost a brother, a brother-in-law, cousins and their husbands, and her father. Her mother lives in Canada. The surviving members of her family are scattered all over the world. Margaret is convinced that only by keeping her children in America can she know for sure that they will be safe and have normal childhoods. She suffers from post-traumatic stress and struggles on a daily basis not to let those bad memories get the upper hand.

Everyday my thoughts turn back to those bad days in Africa. I was very angry for many years. But now, when I find myself getting sad, I remember how I sang to myself as I walked through the jungles and deserts. If there's anything I have learned it is to never give up hope. God saved me and continues to bless me every day.

Chapter Three

Mama Achol

When I heard the plane overhead I looked up. All of a sudden I saw objects falling through the air. They glistened in the sun, and I think all of us were mesmerized for those first few moments. Suddenly, there were huge explosions. Within moments the boat was torn apart, reduced to rubble and floating pieces of burning wood.

Mama Achol's Story

Achol Kuek Atem and her daughters live in Garland, Texas. Mama not only carried her own three children out of Sudan, she carried her sister's children out as well. Her story is as follows:

We lived in Malakal, which is a capital city in the upper Nile. The year was 1984, and for some time we had been hearing rumors of war. Even though I was only twenty-four years old, I knew that once war broke out, the fighting would be very fierce between the North and the South. My husband, who worked for the government, was Minister of Finance and he too felt uneasy. Like any mother, my first concern was for my children. I had two daughters: Awak, who was eight years old, and Ayen, who was one, and a son, Aguer, who was seven.

Both my husband and I decided the children would be much safer with my mother in her village. While my husband stayed in the city, I boarded a ship that would take all of us to our destination. After a few days in my village I boarded the boat heading back to Malakal.

That same day, the ship was bombed. It turned out that the attackers were rebels who would later form the Sudan People's Liberation Army (SPLA). They had mistaken our boat for a troop ship and had no idea it carried civilians.

How can I describe that experience? It was a beautiful day. I was standing by the rail, gazing out at the array of wildlife and birds on the banks of the Nile River. When I heard the plane overhead I looked up. All of a sudden I saw objects falling through the air. They glistened in the sun, and I think all of us were mesmerized for those first few moments. Suddenly, there were huge explosions. Within moments the boat was torn apart, reduced to rubble and floating pieces of burning wood.

Miraculously, I was untouched. I had been standing by the engine which had exploded when the bomb hit, but I was unhurt. I was caught in a puzzle. Even though I had survived the explosion, I was in a very dangerous situation.

I couldn't swim, and I was four months pregnant. Clinging to what was left of the wooden housing of the engine, I prayed.

"God, what can I do? If I stay, I burn. The river is infested with crocodiles, so if I jump into the river, I drown or get torn to pieces." I decided drowning was the best alternative.

My heart told me to jump, so I jumped. I remember fighting to keep my head above water and thrashing around wildly, grasping at any plank that floated my way as the current swept me to shore.

Apparently, God had other plans for me, because I crawled up onto the bank unharmed. I was shaking violently, not only from the cold but also from shock and fear. An amazed on-looker, who had witnessed the entire event, rushed over and wrapped me in a large towel.

I was taken to a small town where I stayed for a month.

Meanwhile, my family had heard about the bombing. Convinced I was dead, they conducted my funeral.

Mama Achol commented that she later heard that it was quite a large and touching affair.

One month later, after learning that there were survivors from the bombing of the ship, the government sent in a helicopter with food and supplies. Another ship was sent to bring us back to the city. I returned to Malakal where I was reunited with my husband. I noticed that the city was strangely quiet. Suddenly there was very little security to be seen anywhere. Our uneasiness increased. A short time later, our worst fears were realized. The military was convinced that the ragtag rebels were hiding in Malakal. The Arabs bombed the city at midnight.

Because of his position my husband was able to secure a helicopter. We flew to my mother's village. My husband, still an employee of the government, was trying to do his job. Even though we were Christians, his hope had been that the Arabs and the Christians could eventually get along. For a long time we had been under pressure because the Arabs were trying to convert us. They offered many enticements, but we, like most of the Sudanese people, would not accept the Muslim's strict Sharia law.

Once we reached the village, my husband made his decision. He left us with my mother and went to Ethiopia, where he joined the SPLA so he could be trained in warfare. Because of his organizational skills he was badly needed.

When the government tried to impose Islamic rule on the southern and western part of Sudan, John Gurang, a charismatic and intelligent individual who is a member of the Dinka tribe, formed the SPLA. Years before, he had come to the United States to attend school in Iowa, where he received his doctorate. I can only assume that, having been educated in the United States, he was unwilling to accept the yoke of slavery the Arabs were trying to force the people of Southern Sudan to accept. He pulled together a large group of outraged and bitter Sudanese who were determined to protect their country and stop the destruction of their homes and the brutal treatment of their people at any cost. A born leader, John was able to transform what had been a loosely knit and disorganized group of inexperienced civilians and mercenary soldiers into a disciplined army. That same army, out of necessity, was supplemented with women and, sometimes, even adolescent soldiers .

The SPLA fought in the second civil war against the Sudanese government which lasted from 1983 to 2005. In 1989, the SPLA joined the National Democratic Alliance. Their aim was to establish a democratic Sudan by putting the National Democratic Alliance in control of the southern part of the country.

In the mid '90s, the SPLA split into two factions and turned on each other. The civilians paid a heavy price.

Described in religious and ethnic terms, the war has also involved a struggle for control of the water and oil resources in the southern and western part of Sudan.

The Arabs, by this time, made their intentions clear. Word spread rapidly that they were attacking and burning the villages, killing all of the boys and men, kidnapping and raping the women, and even killing the children. Systematically, they murdered everyone they found.

I had been in the village for two months when they attacked. When I heard the first gunfire, I knew we had to get to the refugee camp in Ethiopia. I immediately began gathering some grain and putting water in as many plastic containers as I could find. I tied them to a rope and hung them around my waist. I wrapped everything in a bundle and put it on my head. My sister, who was pregnant, ran with my mother into the brush. Along with my children, I took her five-year-old son and her daughters, who were four and six. I carried the smaller ones on my back.

The Sahara desert is a deadly place. The sun cooks you during the day, and the nights are very cold. By the time we got to the edge of this barren landscape, we had joined a large group of people. Because of the heat, we walked at night and slept during the day, wherever we could find a sliver of shade.

In the village, our people have always been very healthy. It would be this health that would carry many of us through. Unfortunately, not all of us made it. Lions and hyenas devoured those who became too sick or weak. Gangs of outlaws and militant Arabs murdered many others.

In the desert, danger is everywhere. You have to be on the lookout for snakes and scorpions. But even though I was frightened, I refused to allow myself to think about these many terrible things. I was determined to get the children to safety.

There are many varieties of scorpions in the deserts and scrublands of Northern Africa. The sting is usually painful, but not deadly.

However, the Yellow Fattail Scorpion carries venom powerful enough to kill a full-grown man in less than two hours if not treated with antivenin.

Sometimes I had to trick the children to keep them walking. They cried and cried. Occasionally they would sit down and refuse to budge. Then I would have to sit down and talk to them.

"See that dead body over there?" I would ask. (There were many.) "Do you want to be like that? Did you hear the lions roar? I think they are very close. In fact, not too long ago, I think I saw two yellow eyes. They were very big! I know you don't want the lions to eat you. You have to keep walking."

As the children listened to me, their eyes would get bigger. They would get up and start walking, faster than before.

When my people are in a desperate situation like this, they share everything. When you lay down, if you have an extra sheet, you give it to someone who doesn't have one. Whatever grain you can spare you give to someone else.

Mama Achol made it to the refugee camp in Ethiopia which was huge and actually consisted of small camps and two larger camps. She was amazed that she had made it through that dangerous seven-day trek through the desert and credits God with bringing her and the children to safety. She and the children adapted to life in the camp, which was not easy. But at least she felt safe. But that safety didn't last because, early one morning in 1991, the Arabs attacked the camp.

People in security had warned us they had heard rumors that we would all have to leave. When the attack finally happened, there were bombs first which were followed by the Arabs who came in on the ground driving jeeps and tanks. They began shooting people and setting everything on fire. When I saw people running I knew it could only get worse. I grabbed the children and, with many others, rushed to the river. Somehow I managed to find a small, narrow boat. Sitting down, I was able to get a couple of the children in the boat with me, but there wasn't enough room for my son. Being a strong swimmer, he swam next to the boat guiding it to shore.

"Don't let go," I yelled. "Stay by the boat."

I saw many of the boats tipping over, spilling people into the water where they were immediately pulled under by crocodiles. I could see the blood exploding out of people's heads as the bullets hit them. Some people, even after they got shot, kept on running.

I was very proud of my son that day. He swam back and forth guiding that boat, helping others make it to shore.

Again we found ourselves trudging wearily along in the desert as we made our way back into Sudan. We soon came to the small city of Akoba.

The people of this city were from the Nucr tribe, and some of its people were refugees also. My friend, who lived in Akoba, had been told by people walking ahead of me that I was coming. She milked her cows and prepared food to give us when we arrived. She was so kind.

"Stay," she pleaded. "You will be safe here."

I was tempted, but then her husband's friend came to visit me.

"You can't stay," he said. "It is too dangerous."

Just as we were leaving, the Arabs raced into Akoba in their jeeps brandishing their guns. To my horror, they caught my brother. Because he was educated they tortured him, trying to force him to tell them where people were hiding. They hacked him into pieces, little by little, until he died.

My sister's husband was buried alive. Almost all of the residents in that village were murdered, including the woman who was my friend. Even her children were killed. We had had such a wonderful friendship over the years. We did everything together. I was heartsick.

When we left Bor, we traveled without stopping from 1990 to 1991 until we came to Kenya. At one point I carried my daughters on my back and dragged my son by his arm through a flood. Floods are common during the rainy season, and they can be very dangerous.

Finally, I was reunited with my husband in Torit. At first all we could do was gaze at each other's beloved face. We could not believe we had survived.

One of the women I knew, who is still in the refugee camp today, had her leg chopped off during the same raid when the Arabs killed my brother. I can't imagine how she managed to live, but she was one of the few who made it out alive.

Through the grace of God, I was able to bring my children to America.

In my lifetime, I have seen many bad things. When I try to understand war, I think it happens when people are not educated. It's then that a country is vulnerable. When I came to American

I could not speak English. I badly wanted an education, but my girls had to come first. I wanted to go to school, but my husband went instead. I want things to be different for my daughters. I tell their suitors that my girls will be educated. I want them all to have college degrees before they get married.

Mama Achol's husband is back in Sudan where he has his old job as Minister of Finance. He tells Mama Achol that the city has been reduced to rubble.

"People go to their jobs and often work three months before they get paid," he says. "Then they'll work another three months before they get paid again."

Yet he, like so many people in Sudan, is determined to rebuild his country and help the Sudanese obtain their independence.

When I interviewed Mama Achol she was dressed in black. I learned that she was in mourning over the loss of Aguer, her first-born son—the same little boy she had led by the hand through the desert. That brave child who had swum across the river, guiding the small boat through the raging water and terrifying slaughter that day on the Gilo river, had grown into a handsome, sincere young man who was loved by all. He loved to read the Bible and was known to give impromptu talks and sermons.

His sister Awok said, "Because my father was gone, Aguer was not only our older brother, he was a father figure for my sister and myself. He was the one who encouraged and advised us. He insisted that we go to school, and he was instrumental in my sister Grace's choice to become a teacher. He was a wonderful role model."

At one point Aguer was diagnosed with bipolar disorder. Mama Achol is still baffled by this because he never lost his temper. Yet, like many refugees, he more than likely suffered from depression. Many psychiatrists claim that refugees from Sudan are some of the most traumatized people in the world.

In February 2007, Aguer, who was still single at the age of 27, decided it was time to get out on his own. He checked into a hotel, and on the phone later, told his father how excited he was about making plans to get an apartment.

When Mama Achol hadn't heard from him in a few days, she grew anxious and called the hotel. The manager went into his room and found Aguer dead. He was lying on the bed, his eyes were closed, and he looked so peaceful it was hard to believe he was not sleeping. Despite the autopsy, there is no known cause of death.

Chapter Four

Awak Bior

When we reached New York, we saw many people of many different nationalities. Some were light-skinned, and some like us were black. But the most shocking thing of all was seeing people who were white. Many of them were Russians. They all spoke many different languages, and like us they were refugees. Who could have imagined that white people could be refugees? Until that point, we had believed that all of the refugees in the world were only black Sudanese people.

Awak Bior's Story

Awak Deng Bor is Mama Achol's oldest daughter. She is 27 years old and was 15 years old when she arrived in New York before coming to Texas. When one of her best friends married a young man who was diagnosed with AIDS, Awak decided she wanted to become a doctor so she could help find a cure for the deadly HIV virus. She has earned a degree in biology and is going to school so that she can get a job with a pharmaceutical company.

This is her story:

My earliest memories are of being with my auntie and my sister, Nyibol, along with my three cousins. I was probably only seven years old at the time. I remember my mother leaving me with my grandmother. I cried and cried.

Hoping she would appear, weeks later I would still go to the road and wait. I think I stayed with both my auntie and my grandmother for a period of two years. My Grandmother babied me. She would ask me from time to time. "Awakcuerdit, do you like staying with me?"

"I love you so much and I love staying with you as long as you keep feeding me with milk, sweet awalwala and corns," I would answer. She would smile and hug me. She never said the words, "I love you," but I could feel how much she loved me and Nyibol.

Life was good then. I was living with people who loved me. There were rumors of war. Because I was a child I didn't care, but the one thing that scared me to death was the sound of guns.

There was a lady who lived with my grandma for a brief time. She would wake up every morning, cook breakfast, put it in a small container and start walking towards the sound of guns. I never understood where she was taking the food and wondered why she liked the sound of guns so much.

Years later, when I was grown, I found out her husband was one of the prisoners awaiting his death.

One day I realized war really was coming because my auntie came and got me and Nyibol from my grandmother's house and we headed for Ethiopia.

It was so hot. I felt like my feet were going to burst into flames. Sometimes, I think this is why I have black spots on my feet. We made it to the Panyidu refugee camp where we joined my uncle, Deng Kuck. He welcomed us with open arms and the next morning we were driven to my mother's camp. When I saw her I ran and kissed her and sat on her lap like a baby.

Life was good in Ehiopia until the day my father was arrested. For five years we lived in fear of getting the news that he was one of the ones who had been chosen to die. He had a broad mind and was always the one to say exactly what he felt. For Sudanese politics, this is not always a good thing.

I remember a day when there was a lot of noise. People were running around everywhere. They would just drop things and run. There was screaming, blood, smoke, shouting and the sounds of gunfire. Mothers were crying, children were dying and fathers were staying behind to fight and to be killed. There was no time to pack. Food, water, clothing, everything was left behind. We just grabbed anything we could put our hands on.

Then I remember walking. My brother and my cousin carried food. It was my job to carry the blankets. Nyibol was barely able to walk, but I believe even she had to carry something. We walked for two months, but they seemed like years. Only God knows how we made it because there is no way anyone could survive that walk. During the day we were so tired we would sit or lie down anywhere and fall asleep. If you heard a gun go off, you just ran. We walked through a dangerous Nuer village. The Arabs influenced them and they often attacked us. Even though they had been our neighbors and looked just like us, except for the tribal markings on their foreheads, they became our enemies.

I began to believe there was a strange disease that infected every being who was after us. The universe had turned against us and we were running. I prayed that I would die before I got caught. You are only nine, you are running and thorn trees are hurting you. You hide in trees with tears pouring down your face as you watch family members and friends being killed. Then you blame yourself for not saving your friend. People who look just like you want to kill you. Girls are being raped. "What is better?" I asked myself. "Dying or torture? Dying takes away all of the pain."

But, I kept walking because of my mother.

We made it to Torit where my mother had to struggle to survive. I heard my mom's friend tell her "Achol, I hear your husband is here in Torit. They are being put in this place in the

43

middle of the forest. Some of them will be released."

My mother knew my father was not coming out. At first she was right. The men who were released were afraid to come and see my mom, but the Man Above can work wonders. My uncle, who was in charge of Torit, was a powerful man and he intervened. My father returned and when he walked in the door, we hugged and kissed him, again and again.

I was older when our family had to run from Torit. When the Arabs attacked, they singled my handsome uncle out and tortured him by hacking him to pieces. People said they did this to try and force him to tell where important people were. It is something that I cannot talk about because that memory always makes me cry.

Again, we were walking and crying. I remember Momma saying over and over, "Keep going, this is not going to end. Just keep going."

My grandma did not want to come, but Momma finally convinced her. I am very glad, for I think she helped save our lives. She had made ghee oil (a liquid made from cheese). Everyday she would give each of us a teaspoon full of this oil and it made us strong.

I remember reaching another city only to find out that the Arabs were already there. We rushed to our uncle's house on the outskirts of town. He had a car and was carrying people away from danger. At first, there was a crowd of people waiting for their turn to ride in that car. Finally, the crowd dwindled until there was no one left but me, my brother and my mom. When the car returned we got in. It was so crowded with people my body was hanging halfway out of the door. To make matters worse, someone was sitting on my head. My brother, Agner, grabbed my arm and never let go, even when I was throwing up. He kept me from falling out.

There were no roads where my uncle was driving, so it was a very rough ride. He was driving very fast.

Finally, we came to a very pretty place by the river. My uncle stopped and left us there. Relieved to be out of the car, we all sat there quietly. I think my mom was trying to think of what we should do next. Suddenly, another car appeared. The passenger in the car was a lady. When she saw Agner she made the driver stop. They knew each other and she pleaded with us to come with her. She told us that all of the people in Torit who were behind us had been killed by the Arabs. We were very sad. Agner told her to go on because God would take care of us.

My brother was right because God did take care of us. My father, who had been walking for miles, found us. When we saw him coming across the horizon, we cried with joy.

As we continued walking we found fruit to eat, so we were not hungry. Everything was green and beautiful, but there was danger. The tribes in that area were very primitive and hostile. The Arabs had paid them to kill us, so we had to be very careful.

The Murle, cooperating with the Arabs, have been hostile towards the Dinka tribe for years. The Arabs encourage hostilities between the tribes in Sudan, by providing arms and money. They know the easiest way to weaken an enemy is to 'divide and conquer.'

We ran to another camp. When it was attacked, we ran again.

"Awak, keep walking," my father said. "You have a strong heart."

I wanted to make him proud, but in my heart I knew I was walking fast because I was terrified. My sister, who was younger, didn't want to walk. She was too little to understand the danger.

I heard stories about young girls in the villages who were kidnapped by the Arabs. If they did not kill them, the Arabs forced them to become their wives. They would be taken away to the desert, never to be seen by their families again.

We finally reached Kakuma, the refugee camp in Kenya. We were among the first arrivals. My father was determined that we would be educated so once we had settled in and registered with the United Nations, he and his brother began to teach everyday how to read.

Finally, our whole family was allowed to come to America. We had dreamed of this time for many months and we were excited.

When we reached New York we saw many people of many different nationalities. Some were light-skinned and some, like us, were black.

But the most shocking thing of all was seeing people who were white.

Many of them were Russians. They spoke many different languages and, like us, they were refugees. Who could imagine that white people could be refugees? Until that point, we had believed that only the black Sudanese people were refugees.

I was sixteen when I enrolled in school in Dallas. I had to jump from the 5th grade to the 9th. It was very confusing. We then moved and I later graduated from highschool.

There are many things I love about this country. Someday I hope to be a doctor, and because I am in America, I know this dream can come true.

I thank God for bringing me to America and providing me with everything. I thank him everyday, but I also ask him, "why?" Why didn't he protect us emotionally? Why can't I forget the war? Why am I so depressed in a country where you can be who you want to be? Why is it, only a few of us get a break? I ask my creator, "why?" My 'whys' are so many I know I have to give them up and count my blessings and thank God for what he has given me.

Awak still carries deep scars from what she witnessed and experienced in Sudan. She is haunted by the vision of the Arabs torturing and dismembering her uncle. Fortunately, she had a lot of family support, coupled with her determination to succeed in life. Typical of those who have seen their mother country destroyed, she has a deep appreciation of America and the generosity and kindness of the American spirit.

Chapter Five

Nyibol Bior

I had been walking for a very long time when I closed my eyes and suddenly had a vision. I saw a mountain with many beautiful houses just up ahead. "Maybe it's white people camping out," I thought.

The next thing I knew, I was there. They were overjoyed to see me. They gave me food, gently washed me, and, with great tenderness, tucked me into bed. I was comforted as I drifted off to sleep, but too soon the vision faded. I woke up to grim reality.

Nyibol Bior's Story

Nyibol is also Mama Achol's daughter. She is single and teaches physical education at Sunset High School, where she is also an assistant coach. On the weekends she works part-time at Starbucks. Even though she was very young at the time her family had to flee Sudan, she has vivid memories. Her story is as follows:

I was very little, and I remember living with my grandmother in a village. I didn't realize at the time that my mother was in the refugee camp in Ethiopia. I remember walking with my Auntie and her children towards Ethiopia, when a truck driven by soldiers who were with the SPLA stopped to pick us up. They put us in the back of the truck with a lot of other people. It was amazing how many people were on that truck. They hung onto anything they could get their hands on. Some curled up, clinging to the undersides of the truck, others fought to grab a railing on the roof of the cab. It was very uncomfortable and before long I was throwing up. Yet, as bad as it was, I somehow knew we were lucky that the SPLA had come along.

When we reached the camp in Ethiopia, my family was reunited. There was little food or water, but finally, we were together.

It was some time later that the camp was attacked. I remember everyone rushing to the river, crying and screaming. There were bullets flying through the air and people falling down, right and left. I can still shut my eyes and see the bodies of dead people floating in the river as I sat with my mother in a boat, with my brother in the water helping us across.

Again, we were running. By now I was old enough to help carry the supplies. I was very scared. Yet, I tried to keep my spirits up and keep up with the adults.

When we reached our village, our grandma was overjoyed to see us. But the Arabs attacked and we had to run again. I was barefoot, and I felt like my feet were on fire.

I look back now and realize that at one point I was so tired and exhausted I was almost walking in my sleep. It was during this time that a very strange thing happened. I had been walking for a long time when I closed my eyes and suddenly had a vision.

I saw a mountain with many beautiful houses just up ahead. "Maybe it's white people camping out," I thought.

The next thing I knew, I was there. They were overjoyed to see me. They gave me food, gently washed me, and, with great tenderness, they tucked me into bed. I was comforted as I drifted off to sleep, but too soon the vision faded. I woke up to grim reality.

The Arabs attacked us again and again. Their planes would swoop down and they would drop their terrible bombs. We dreaded that sound. All you could do was throw yourself down in the dirt and pray that it was not your time to die. We moved at night, and we could not cook food when it was dark because the Arabs would see our fires.

We made it to Camp Kakuma in Kenya before the UN had arrived. The first thing my father did was build a house. But we didn't stay in the camp very long. Instead we went to Nirobi, Kenya, where we lived for four years and I attended primary school. It was difficult since I didn't speak Swahili, which is the language used in Kenya. Even though I was ten years old I was put in the first grade. I, along with most of my family, am tall and the children made fun of me. I was very embarrassed. By the time I got to the fourth grade I was second in my class.

The people in Kenya did not like the idea of people coming there without documentation. The police began rounding up and arresting people who didn't have passports. We spent a lot of time hiding in our house, and when we would hear someone knocking we would send my sister Grace to open the door. Because of her lighter complexion, the police would take one look at her and assume she was a native.

I was fourteen years old when we came to Texas. I couldn't understand what anyone said. The kids saw me as someone who was very different, and for a long time I didn't have any friends. By nature, I am a talkative, friendly person. I would stand in line at the cafeteria, and when I saw someone sitting alone at a table, I would just sit down and act like we already knew each other. Some days, I just didn't have the courage, and it was on these days I hid in the bathroom until lunch was over. I was very lonely.

Because of my limited English, I was put in a classroom with Vietnamese-and Spanish-speaking kids. Since I couldn't under-stand anyone, I paid compete attention to the teacher. By the time I was in the ninth grade I was back in regular classes. I made the basketball team and built a good relationship with the coach. I made varsity in my sophomore year.

My coach was my inspiration. I owe her a lot. Now I am a teacher, and I get frustrated because I see so many American kids that don't realize how lucky they are and appreciate what they have. Because of what I've seen in war, I am grateful for the opportunities this country offers. I know I can make it. I tell my students that all they have to do is try.

After I develop my career, I want to go back and contribute to the people in Africa. But America is my adopted country. I am here because God was my guidance. He still is.

Chapter Six

Rebecca Alier

Having survived our ordeal, over the many years of walking, we were skeletal and emaciated. When the UN workers came into the camp with food and water we were overjoyed. We stared at these strangers, momentarily transfixed. Were they angels? We had never seen a white person before. Suddenly we just wanted to touch them, to feel them. We wanted to see if they were real. As we rushed forward with arms outstretched, it was too much for them. They ran away.

Rebecca Alier's Story

Rebecca Alier is the mother of three little girls. Born in Bor, she is not sure how old she is and does not know when she was born. She was a toddler when her town was raided. As an infant, Rebecca came down with tuberculosis of the spine, which left her upper body deformed. She is convinced that only through God's grace is she alive today. Her story is as follows:

When our town was attacked, a bigger child picked me up as he ran into the jungle. When he got tired he put me down. A little later another big child came along, picked me up, and carried me until he got tired. This went on day after day and week after week until I could walk on my own. I found myself in a group of about twenty-five children, mostly boys, along with a few older girls. They became my family. They shared what little food and water they had. Before they escaped, some of the older children had managed to wrap some grain in bundles which they carried on their heads. By chewing on the kernels we could produce saliva. Often there was no food and no water, so there were days when we were dehydrated and starving. It was during these desperate times that we were forced to resort to drinking our own urine. Even this can be a problem because, if you are dehydrated, it is hard to go to the bathroom. Sometimes you can only force out a few drops. Often we walked at night. There is a tree in Africa that has a sweet thick liquid in the bark. When we found one of these trees we felt very lucky. There is another tree that has a tiny fruit. Before the fruit is fully ripe it is so hot it will make tears stream from your eyes. When the fruit is fully ripe it is delicious. When we found one of those trees, the bigger girls would climb to the top to get the riper fruit. I would stand underneath with my hands cupped. "Just give me a little," I would plead. Sometimes, out of desperation, I would find fruit that was not ripe on the ground. When the other children saw tears streaming down my face as I ate the fruit, they could not keep from laughing. Then there was a plant that was highly poisonous if you ate it uncooked. You had to cook it for hours. One day, I was so hungry that I fished a piece out of our cooking pot before it was time. "It is probably just fine," I told myself. When I ate it I passed out. But again, God let me live.

I had no idea where we were going and, I suspect, few of us did. I remember a desperate desire to stay with my adopted family, so I struggled hard to keep up. They were all I had. Also, because a few of us were so small, the going was slow. When we came to a big tree it was our shelter, but it was dangerous because large snakes also like to be in big trees. For some reason, even when we saw snakes, they never bothered me.

I was walking one day when a strange animal started walking beside me. "What a lovely goat," I thought, thumping it on the back. "You are a very lovely goat," I said. "I wonder what you are doing here." The animal leaned over and licked my hand as we walked along comfortably for some time. Suddenly I heard a big girl scream.

"Rebecca, run!"

"Why?" I replied. "It's just a goat."

"No it is not a goat! It's a hyena, and it wants to eat you."

Suddenly my heart was beating very fast. Quickening my step, I looked over at my newfound friend, the goat. I realized it had very long teeth. It sat down in the path and watched me as I hurried away. Maybe it was trying to decide if it should eat me for dinner.

The hyena is Africa's most common carnivore. It will hunt in packs or alone. This meat eater has very powerful jaws and can be very bold when hungry. It has been known to attack people when they are asleep in their huts. When a hyena attacks a human, it attacks the face first.

I saw many dead people during those years. The longer a person is dead, the more horrifying the body becomes because it swells up. I almost became one of those dead bodies. One time, I stepped on a thorn that went deep into my foot. I had a hard time walking as it was, and this made it even more difficult. It was very painful. Another time, I became so weak I couldn't walk. I fell down and cut my leg. It was a deep cut, and I was bleeding badly. I didn't think I would be able to go on. Then someone sat down by my side, managed to produce a scrap of cloth, and stopped the bleeding. I bear a jagged scar to this day.

I had another close encounter that proved again God had a special plan for me. Still a little girl, I was sitting alone in the dirt when a huge snake slithered out of the grass and began to move around me in a circle. It was yellow with a patch of black under its jaw. Once it had completed a ring with me sitting in the center, it reared up until its head was at eye level, staring directly into my eyes. I sat motionless. Suddenly I heard one of the big boys yell, "Look at Rebecca. It's a constrictor, and it will swallow her. We have to get her out of there."

Grabbing huge branches, all of the boys began to beat on the snake, but it would not budge. The width of its body was the size of a large tree. Then after many minutes of staring fixedly at me with glittering eyes, it suddenly lowered its head and died.

There are more than ten varieties of venomous snakes in Africa, some of them measuring up to twelve feet or more in length. This species includes the Black Mamba, Saw-scaled Viper, and the majestic Egyptian Cobra. A constrictor does not have a venomous bite but will lunge and sink its teeth into its prey, then wrap itself around the body, crushing the bones and asphyxiating the victim. The snake then swallows its prey whole.

Rebecca was told later that her parents were Christians, but her grandparents were animists. They worshiped Nhialic, the creator god. Rebecca's forefathers believed that if a member of the family lost faith in their religion and encountered their token animal, they would either be eaten immediately or the animal would choose to die.

When we arrived at the refugee camp, I was amazed. I couldn't comprehend any other life than what I had endured for so many years. We were accustomed to living with many fears. Fears of soldiers, bombs, bullets, light-skinned devils on horseback, wild animals, thirst, and hunger—all of these things had become our normal existence. For me, and many others, it was all we had ever known. We had been walking, walking, day after day, then suddenly we were in this huge crowd of people and we no longer needed to walk. I didn't know what to do. I knew I had to be someone's little girl, but where were they? Then an older boy came up to me and announced, "I am your cousin. I will take care of you." And he did.

Not long after our arrival people from the United Nations came. The first thing we saw was a series of white trucks driving toward the gates of the camps. At first the trucks looked like mirages as they shimmered in the searing heat. We gathered at the entrance, staring. Many of us had never seen a vehicle. When the UN workers got out of the trucks with food and water we were overjoyed.

Having survived our ordeal over our many years of walking, we were skeletal and emaciated. Transfixed at first, all we could do was stare at these strangers. Were they angels? We had never seen a white person before. Suddenly we just wanted to touch them, to feel them, to see if they were real. We rushed forward with arms outstretched; it was too much for them. They ran away.

We soon discovered that, like us, the UN workers were human and realized that they were trying their best to help all of us. They gave each one of us one cup of corn, one head of cabbage, a cup of beans, and a cup of oil. To us it was like being given a fortune. Reality didn't dawn on us at first that these supplies had to last a whole month. But best of all, the UN brought clothes. The problem was size. Everyone was given a shirt, underwear, socks, shoes, and a pair of shorts or pants for the men or a skirt for the women. Since there was only one set of clothing for each person, if it didn't fit, you were in trouble. Luckily for me, I was so skinny it didn't matter. No matter how little something was, it fit. The UN also gave us plastic tarps for shelter. They then drilled a well and showed us how to turn on the tap for fresh water. It was like a miracle. Each day we would stand in line, waiting our turn. It filled our hearts with joy just seeing that clean water flowing into our containers.

Then I met another boy. His name was Jacob, and he told me that when I was old enough we would get married. This made my cousin very angry because my suitor did not have the bride price. I attended church on a regular basis, and my new admirer would always follow. He too had lost his entire family.

"Don't be mad at Jacob," I told my cousin. "He can't help it because he has nothing. None of us have anything."

When Rebecca came to Houston she was the first Lost Girl to arrive in Texas. Fifteen years old and pregnant, she was desperate to reunite with Jacob Deng, the Lost Boy who was her admirer in the refugee camp and also the father of her child. He had ended up in Arizona. When he came to visit, he passed through Dallas and decided it was the ideal place for them to live. Rebecca laughs when she remembers what things were like when she came to the United States.

The only words in English I could say were "ok", "yes", and "no." My cousin told me my birthday is January 1st. You'd be surprised how many people from Sudan were supposedly born on January 1st, but I never forget to celebrate my birthday. When I inquired about school, I was told that since I was fifteen years old, I would have to enroll in high school as a sophomore. How could I do this when I had not even attended the first grade? I could not even count.

I remember my teens being especially hard. There was not a mother or older sister to teach me how to be a woman. I was very naïve. I was also very shy. At times I blamed myself for not having a mother, and at other times I blamed my mother, wondering if she had deserted me.

Describing her life as a series of ups and downs, Rebecca bears a heavy burden: the tragic loss of her five-year old son.

My son woke up one morning and told me he had had a very bad dream. He said that in the dream he had fallen out of the window in his room, and when he looked up he was looking through a pool of blood. His father assured him that we would move the bed away from the window. We went to church as usual, but I forgot to tell the minister about my son's dream. Later that day, a friend called and asked me to bring the children over to play with her children. When I went to visit, my son and daughter, along with the woman's older children, went outside. My daughter told me later that my son jumped into the pool. The older children said they thought he could swim. When my daughter ran in and told me I ran outside. We got him out and he was still breathing, but he died in the ambulance while he was being transferred to Cooke Hospital in Fort Worth.

Rebecca not only lost her son that day, Child Protective Services came and took Amy, her three-year old daughter. Rebecca remembers her bewilderment when she was told this was standard procedure when something like this occurred. She feels her lack of education and inability to communicate in English worked against her horribly in that situation. An attorney allowed her to pay a small fee weekly out of her paycheck as he handled her case, and in the weeks to come, she spent so much time attending parenting classes she lost her job. Six months later, the judge gave her back her daughter. After several unannounced visits, the social workers from CPS decided she was, after all, a good parent.

When Rebecca's third child was born she named her Ruth, after her mother, who she assumed was dead. A few days after Ruth was born, Rebecca got a phone call from the refugee camp in Kenya. It was her mother.

At first I did not believe it. I thought she was trying to trick me. She told me people in the refugee camp had told her she had a daughter who had gone to America.

"Listen to my voice," my mother said. "Can't you hear how much we sound alike?" Then she began to tell me the nicknames and names of endearment she called me when I was just a baby, and I began to remember. We both cried and cried. I found out my grandma and all five of my brothers and sisters were killed the night the Arabs attacked. My mother told me that when she couldn't find me, she and another woman had run into the jungle during the attack. The other woman took her baby with her. When the baby cried the Arabs found them both, along with some other people who were hiding. Some of the women were angry because the woman had brought her baby, but Rebecca's mother defended her. "She can't help it. She's a mother. Babies can't help it. They are like angels. They are innocent."

The Arabs killed the baby and its mother, but Rebecca's mother was used as a slave to carry the soldiers' weapons.

"If you didn't do what the Arabs told you to do, they would kill you instantly," she told Rebecca. Chained and carrying a heavy burden, she never complained. Day after grueling day, her mother looked straight ahead as she walked. She always did what she was told. Even children were used as beasts of burden.

Then, miraculously, when the Arabs were near the place they were headed, they released her. She almost died in the desert before she came to a village where a kind woman nursed her back to health and helped her get to the refugee camp. This same woman, with the help of the Red Cross, helped her locate Rebecca.

Don't be angry at me, Rebecca," her mother said toward the end of their conversation. "It's no one's fault. It's the war."

In the Dinka tribe, it is the custom to name children after deceased family members so the relatives will not be forgotten. It is also considered bad luck to name a child after a living relative. Rebecca's mother convinced her that naming the baby Ruth was not bad luck but, in this case, good luck. Rebecca agrees since it was only after the baby was born that she found out her mother was still alive.

Rebecca's greatest desire is to bring her mother to America. She has filled out forms, only to be told later they were the wrong forms. Now her mother is on a list, but Rebecca has been told it will be a long time. It has already been nine months. Rebecca is afraid her mother will die in the refugee camp and there will not be anyone in the camp to bury her.

Rebecca suspects her mother was raped, but it is a sensitive subject that is not discussed. Women in Africa feel a deep sense of shame when they are raped. They will usually only say that the Arabs beat them. The Arab soldiers and Janjaweed have a diabolical aim when they commit rape. They know that it is an effective way to destroy the family unit. Often the men leave, and the women are forced to bear the shame, which leaves deep psychological scars for the rest of their lives.

"I always smile," Rebecca says. "I'm a very happy person. I know when I die I will be with my son, and I know he watches over me. Even though my life has been full of ups and downs, in many ways I have led a charmed life. The memories of those terrible years in Sudan are blurry in my mind, but I still have bad dreams. I'm amazed that any of us lived. I still marvel at those brave older children who did not abandon me to die but cared for me even when their lives were at risk. God answered my prayers. I have found my mother and I have my own family. I pray to God every day. Part of my prayer is always the same."

"Please God, do not let the Arabs take America. Just let it be Sudan. These people in America have good hearts. If not for America where would we be? This country is a blessing."

Chapter Seven

Kuei Mading

When I first arrived in Mississippi, I stayed with a lady named Bobbi Stack. Upon walking into her home for the first time, a strange little animal ran up to me, barking. It seemed quite ferocious and fearsome. I was very frightened.

"Mommie," I said. "That animal is very scary. It looks like a cat but barks like a dog. What is it?"

"It's a Pomeranian," she answered.

Kuei Mading's Story

When Kuei Mading arrived in Mississippi in 2000 she was seventeen years old. Kuei works for a computer company and loves her job. Her husband works at the airport. When she first arrived a Catholic charity placed her with Bobbi Stack. In Sudan, all older women are called "Momma" or "Mommie." Her story is as follows:

During my childhood, I never knew anything other than war. I lived in Bor, and in 1989 the Arabs attacked my village. It was early in the morning, and we were all sleeping. First there were the bombs. Then, the soldiers came in on camels and horses. When a soldier shot my mother, I couldn't understand what had happened. I was only seven years old, and when I saw her fall down I threw my arms around her. "Mommy, Mommy, wake up," I cried as I clung to her neck.

Our neighbor, Momma Aker, rushed in and grabbed me. "Don't touch her again," she said. "She is already gone."

Most of the Dinka children had never seen a dead person before the Arabs attacked their villages. Death is a taboo subject, and parents do not talk about death or permit their children to see corpses.

She took my hand and with her seven-year-old son Ajith, we ran into the bush. Soon we joined other survivors and began walking, not realizing we would have to walk for three months.

Wherever we went, the Arabs chased us. They even bombed us on our way to Sopia. Death was everywhere. There was no food. Once we went fourteen days without water. Our feet became very swollen. When you get too thirsty and dehydrated, your heart flutters and your legs become very weak. If you sit down, you die. Some of us were too dehydrated to produce urine. Those who were able to produce it, shared. We shared everything. We knew the animals could smell us. We could hear the lions as they huffed and roared when they caught our scent. The older people would raise their arms and yell. The lion, known as the King of the Jungle, would sometimes just walk away.

It is true that when you are terribly thirsty you can smell water. Like animals, we followed the tantalizing odor and headed towards the river. When we arrived we couldn't contain ourselves, even though we knew it was dangerous. Soldiers could be hiding in the trees, but we were desperate. We drank our fill. The older boys killed a gazelle. While we were eating, I was sitting on a rock ledge next to a woman who was pregnant. Suddenly a shot rang out. The woman fell over dead. Snipers were firing at us. Then a bullet whizzed by me. It was so close it burned the fabric of my blouse. I began to cry hysterically. I thought I was dead. The next thing I remember is everyone standing around me, telling me I was alive and needed to get up. God let me live.

The time came when my neighbor's little boy Ajith and I were simply too weak to go on. Mama Aker would carry Ajith several feet ahead. Then she would put him down, come back, pick me up, and carry me on her back. This went on for some time.

We finally came to a big tree. This is where I found my sister who had been running in another group. We were both relieved that we were still alive. "Why do they hate us?" I asked.

"Because the Arabs are Muslims and we are Christians," I was told.

I was very confused.

Many died from thirst. I thought I would never taste water again. Then God, in His mercy, made it rain. He did His job. I promised Him, that if I lived, I would do something good with my life.

We knew we had reached safety when we arrived at the refugee camp in Ethiopia. Even though food was scarce and conditions were harsh, we thought the worst was over. Then, two years later, at 5 a.m. in the morning, the camp came under attack. The Arabs attacked the good places first, which meant they bombed the hospital. We ran to rescue the sick people. My sister, who had just had a miscarriage, rushed out of the hospital when the bombs started to fall. I met her on the way to the river.

It had rained for hours, and the banks of the Gilo River flooded. The water had overflowed the banks of the river and was up to the adults' thighs. My sister was still very weak, and I was too small to carry her little boy, so I drug him by the arm. As we ran, I saw people crawling on a rope stretched across the river. Suddenly, right in front of me, a cobra reared up and raised its hooded head. I had seen many people die from snakebite, but I was very lucky because suddenly the rain swept it away. A few minutes later we saw it in a tree. Even though it failed to bite me, it bit other people who later died.

The Janjaweed looted the camp, taking all of our food and supplies. Some of the soldiers were hiding in the grass waiting for us at the water. All we could do was run and hope that we would not get hit. In my mind I can still see the hands of people reaching into the air as the river swallowed them up. I saw some people shot by Arabs and others eaten by crocodiles. The old ladies and the babies died first. The tall people put the children on their shoulders as they waded into the water. People were dying all around me. My cousin, who I loved very much, died in that river.

For five months we were on the road to Kenya. We would run at night, sleep a few hours, wake up, and run again. During that time the UN workers came in trucks bringing us water and food. When we became too exhausted to walk, the older people would drag us by our arms. "If you don't walk, you will die," they said. Even when we cried and begged them to let us lie down, they were relentless.

We finally reached the refugee camp in Kenya, where I later would meet my husband in church. We had known each other in Sudan. We prayed together and became inseparable. Miraculously, I also found my father. It was a wonderful reunion. Neither one of us could believe the other one had survived.

My girlfriends and I learned to speak English in the camp's school. We all wanted a better life and decided we wanted to go to America. We knew we had to be careful because, in Africa, women are property. We had foster families. We were unpaid servants, and we represented potential dowries. My girlfriends and I filled out the paperwork without telling anyone. Then, we had to act like everything was normal and wait. One day we found our names on a list. We didn't tell the elders we were leaving until the day before the plane was scheduled to arrive. They were shocked.

At first, I was worried about coming to America. It was a big decision. There were nine girls on the same flight to New York. I was very baffled by the assigned seating. I couldn't understand why we couldn't all sit together. When we arrived in New York it was cold. I had never experienced anything like it. We couldn't stop shivering. We waited a whole day for our connecting flights. No one but me would eat the food. After a few bites, I decided I liked the spaghetti.

When I first arrived in Mississippi, I lived with a lady named Bobbi Stack.

Upon walking into her home for the first time, a strange little animal ran up to me, barking. It seemed quite ferocious and fearsome. I was very frightened.

"Mommie," I said. "This animal is very scary. It looks like a cat but barks like a dog. What is it?"

"It's a Pomeranian."

Bobbi looked at me kindly when she saw my reaction to her funny little dog, but there was a twinkle in her eye. I know now she had to refrain from laughing. She was very kind. She took care of us and complimented me on my English.

Like the other Lost Girls and Lost Boys, Kuei was horrified and shaken by the bombing on 9/11.

I prayed, "Oh my God! We came to America and now this thing is happening again. Where do you want us to go?"

One Lost Boy explained later why the Lost Boys and Girls were so traumatized when the United States was attacked on September 11.

"We had run from war," he said. "America was the last great place for us. Here we knew we would be safe. Everyone can believe anything they want to believe in this country. Americans are good. Then 9/11 happened, and it was as if the whole world was tipping over. In our minds, it was just the beginning of what we had experienced in Sudan—endless bloodshed, suffering, and war."

The Arabs killed my sister, brothers, and kidnapped my cousin who they raped and killed. These were all people I loved, and now they are gone. I have nothing but memories. When I shut my eyes, I can see their faces, I can hear their voices and their laughter. I see the arms reaching out of the river as they drowned before they could save themselves.

As Kuei told me about the horrific ordeals, the painful memories brought tears to her eyes. Yet, like all of the other Lost Girls, she has an incredible resiliency. Almost completely Americanized, she and her husband both work hard and are earning their share of the American dream. Even though this couple has adapted well, there are still things that Kuei finds difficult to get used to. She worries about the chemicals in American food and confides that she doesn't care for sweets. When she is invited to a restaurant, she finds herself overwhelmed by the menu with so many items to choose from. Invariably, she loses her appetite. When I asked her if her husband helped her with their nine-month-old baby boy, this is how she answered:

"When in Rome, do as the Romans do. My husband helps me in every way. He picks the baby up from daycare and does everything he can to help me. We are a team. In America people do things equally. This would never happen in Sudan or Kenya."

Kuei adds, "Someday I would like to go back to Africa. I would like to visit those places that played such a huge role in my life. Africa is a beautiful country. I can never forget it."

Chapter Eight

Mary Kuir

I was only six years old when we finally made it to the refugee camp. Finally we were safe. Then I began having the dream. It was the same thing over and over, night after night. In the dream, I was trying to balance myself on a rope stretched across the Gilo River. Like a trapeze artist in a circus, I was carefully putting one foot in front of the other as I tried not to look at the raging water below. Then I fell. Just before I hit the water I woke up. "It is just a nightmare," I told myself. Or was it?

Mary Kuir's Story

Physically, Mary is typical of the Sudanese people. She is slender and tall and has a beautiful smile. She has a two-year-old son and, as of this writing, had just suffered a miscarriage. She reports that when her husband is not working, he helps take care of their son. He works with computers, and she has just been hired to work at Presbyterian Hospital. Her story is as follows:

I really don't remember much about the attack on our village. I was only six years old at the time. I don't even remember what time of the day it occurred. All I remember is that the big people said we had an enemy and we needed to run. I ran into the forest. I was alone and very frightened. I finally found some of my cousins. We were on foot as we tried to make our way to the city of Bubia. I think we ran day and night for approximately a month. We were just a group of children, comprised of big kids and little kids. During the day, there would be attacks by the Arab tribesmen. We never saw the soldiers because they would hide in the grass. When we realized we were being attacked, it was always too late. Suddenly shots would ring out, people would fall down, and we would all scatter, running as fast as we could.

In the forest, there were many dangerous animals. One day a huge lion leaped down on us. He seemed to come out of nowhere.

His roars seemed to shake the very trees. We all ran, but for one child it was too late. When the lion caught him, he screamed for help, but we could not help him.

Because there was no food and water, a lot of people died. Instinctively, we headed for the river. The thirst was agonizing, and the river was very far away. The bigger people ran ahead and brought water back to us to keep the smaller ones from dying.

We arrived at Pishala in 1991, where we would stay for a year. I was relieved that I had made it safely to the refugee camp. Finally I was safe. Then I began having the dream. It was the same thing over and over, night after night. In the dream, I was trying to balance myself on a rope stretched across the Gilo River. Like a trapeze artist in a circus, I was carefully putting one foot in front of the other as I tried not to look at the raging water below. Then I fell. Just before I hit the water I woke up. "It is just a nightmare," I told myself. Or was it?

Then in 1991, the attack on the camp happened at four o'clock in the afternoon. I remember hearing the bombs, then there was gunfire, and suddenly everyone was running. No one had time to grab anything, and many of us were barefoot. As I ran through a hail of bullets towards the river, there were people falling down all around me. The water was very high, and the current was very strong. I crouched below the side of the bank trying to hide. My heart was pounding. I felt trapped. I was one of those who couldn't swim. Would the Arabs finally kill me, or would I drown? Then some men from the camp swam across the river and tied a large rope around a tree on the other side. As men tied the rope around the tree on this side of the river, I remembered my dream. That nightmare had become a reality. With both hands clasped on the rope and my body hanging over the river, I moved across, one hand at a time. "I am going to die now," I decided. Then, miraculously I found myself on the other side.

Again I was walking, and when I could, I would run. This time my cousins were nowhere to be seen. Instead I found myself with another group of children. "I am all alone," I thought. I think it was then that my heart truly broke. We walked for two days and two nights, and all during that time, the snipers kept shooting at us. All they wanted to do was kill people.

In 1992, we reached the Kakuma camp in Kenya, where I would live for nine years. I met a boy I knew from my village. He had escaped before me. He was two years older. Since we were both children, we had no idea we would someday be married.

On the flight to the United States, I was very frightened. I was afraid the plane would fall out of the air. It took a very long time. I arrived in the United States on December 5, 2000 and was placed with a black family in Mississippi. They mistreated me. When my older cousin tried to call me on the phone, they would not accept his calls. I did not stay for the two-year program but went to live with my cousin.

My husband and I became engaged on the phone. He had come to the United States first, and he had to pay the bride price, which was $15,000 American dollars. During our entire engagement, we only communicated on the phone. During that time, my family in Africa checked him out carefully.

They wanted to make sure he was a nice person and that his relatives were nice as well. All of this had to be done before they would give us their blessing.

We were married on November 27, 2004. Both of us had much in common. We had grown up on our own, from the time we were little children. As for my family, many of them are gone. I only know for sure that the Arabs killed my oldest brother.

When the twin towers were attacked on September 11, 2001, it was a terrible time. "They are still following us, God," I said. "What happened? I thought we left all of that behind."

Life is better here, and I want to stay in America. Someday I would like to go to college so I can become a nurse. I want my son to have an education and to always be free. I am very grateful to the American people because they have given us support. They treat us as equals and have given us a great opportunity. I still have a broken heart, but I thank God that he made my heart strong and that it is getting stronger every day. We are Christians, and this is a country where everyone can follow the religion they prefer.

Even though the memories are painful, Mary told me at the end of the interview that she was glad she was able to tell her story. "It makes me feel better," she said.

Chapter Nine

Elizabeth Aynea

I had big problems with my siblings because there were so many dead people on the ground. When we would stumble over a body, they would panic and try to run away. Finally I found a sheet. I tied all of them to the sheet and led them in a straight line. Of course, they cried. "Where is Mama, I want Mama," I heard over and over again. They were hungry, thirsty, and bewildered. I wanted to cry too, but I didn't. I was the eldest sister, so I tried to act like it was perfectly normal to tie your little brothers and sister to a sheet and lead them through the desert.

Elizabeth Aynea's Story

Elizabeth cannot speak English, so Peter, her brother-in-law, acted as the translator. When he translated her story, he laughed and shook his head in admiration at her bravery and ability to come up with a solution to a problem that few people could have solved. Elizabeth works at Parkland Hospital. Her story is as follows:

We were sleeping when the Arabs attacked. My mother told all six of us to run as fast as we could. "Follow the group," she said. The women were trying to save the children, and the men were trying to defend our village. We people of Sudan feel attached to our land. Many of our elders made the decision then and there that if they had to die, it would be on the ground where they had lived their entire lifetimes. But they wanted us to live, so they told us to run. I would learn later that my father was killed in that attack.

We first headed to the refugee camp, Dimo, which is in Ethiopia. Shortly after we arrived, the camp was attacked with bombs and tanks. We were forced to run again. This time we ran to the town Pachalla, which also came under attack.

We were shocked when we came to the next village because it was deserted. Everyone had run away because they were afraid of the Arabs. It was so strange walking through the village. Where was the laughter of children, the voices of the men and the women, the crying of babies? Where was the barking of the dogs? Instead of the busy life, so typical of our people, and the delicious aromas of cooking food, there was nothing. Even the birds refused to sing. As we walked through the village, I felt that I was in the presence of ghosts who were trying to tell me something but could not come through. For a few minutes I had the strange thought that maybe I had died and this was the afterlife.

Always running, always hungry, thirsty, and scared—this was my life.

When we reached the camp in Kapiot, which is on the border of Kenya, even though there was no food, I was ecstatically happy because I was reunited with my mother and siblings. Just seeing my loved ones brought joy to my heart. We would hold each other and smile, laugh, then cry.

Months later this camp was attacked. This time my mother fled with the other children, while I ran with my uncle. In the desert, someone gave us a car. There was not room for my uncle, so he continued on foot. The driver crammed as many children in the car that could be squeezed in. Driving wildly over the rough terrain, he almost got us to Kapeota when the Arabs dropped a bomb directly onto the car. It was terrible. The driver and some of the children were killed, others were injured, and some just had bruises and scratches. Miraculously, I was unhurt. Dazed, I drug myself out of the wreckage and then reality dawned. I realized I was utterly alone. It was a devastating feeling for a young girl. Numb with despair, I just kept on walking. I could not feel anything, and by this time, I could not even cry. Yet, God is great in His infinite wisdom, because somehow I managed to walk to the camp in Kapeota, where God gave me yet another miracle. I was reunited with my mother and siblings. It was a joy to see them again. When I told them about riding in the car and being bombed from the air, they were amazed. We never saw my uncle again.

In 1992, the worst attack of all happened in Kapeota. First there were the bombs. Then government troops moved in with tanks. The elders told us later that they attacked the camp because they had suffered heavy losses in a fierce battles with the SPLA (Sudan's People Liberation Army). This was how they retaliated.

This time, when we fled, my mother had only been able to grab one of us before she ran away. I had the other four. All of us were barefoot. We were on our own in a very dangerous area. The local people who lived around Kapeota were very primitive. They were killing and robbing the refugees. Sometimes people were in such panic that they would run right into a thorn bush and just keep on running. The barbs on these bushes are so long and sharp they can take out your eye or tear off a piece off flesh. It was not unusual for us to see pieces of flesh hanging from the tree along with human eyeballs impaled on the branches.

Then there were the land mines. The Arabs are clever and cunning. It is amazing how they make these bombs. Some are designed to blow up vehicles, and others are designed to kill people. Some are so sensitive a bird can set them off.

As a twelve-year-old girl, I had to be very careful. I knew that I could be raped and killed if I were caught. I was being hunted like an animal. I was the big sister, but now I had to be the mother because I was the eldest and had to take care of my brothers and sister. I had always been my mother's helper, so my siblings tried to obey me the best that they could. We would stay very still and quiet as I listened for the sound of gunfire and explosions. Then I would guide all of them very carefully in a different direction.

My biggest problem was due to the dead people on the ground. When we would stumble over a body, my little brothers and sister would panic and try to run away. There were many dead bodies so it happened again and again. I would have to catch the little ones and calm them down, and I had to keep them quiet. As little as they were, instinctively, they were horrified at the sight of death. Then I found a sheet. I tied all of them to the sheet and led them in a line. Of course, they cried. "Where is mama, I want mama," I heard over and over. They were hungry, thirsty, and bewildered. I wanted to cry too, but I didn't. I was the eldest sister, so I tried to act like it was perfectly normal to tie your little brothers and sister to a sheet and lead them through the desert.

The nights were the worst. We would lie huddled together. I would tell them everything was fine, but I knew this was not true. It is very hard taking care of children when you do not have shelter and they are hungry and tired. I knew there were wild animals prowling around looking for food. We were weak from hunger, and we were exhausted. I knew we were easy prey for lions and hyenas.

Because it was May, some of the trees bore fruit. There were also strange plants. Some were good, but some were poisonous.

When you get desperate, you will eat or drink anything. If you could cook some of the plants, that was better. Eaten raw, they could make you sick or even kill you. We walked for two weeks before we reached the refugee camp in Kenya. I think even the other refugees were amazed when they saw me leading my little brothers and sister into the camp by a sheet.

When Elizabeth reached the refugee camp in Kenya, she could finally stop running. She found her paternal aunt, who immediately took charge of her and her siblings. A few years later, Elizabeth met her husband Simon in the camp and they were married. Along with their children, they came to Texas in June of 2006. Very few married couples are allowed to leave the refugee camps, so Elizabeth and her husband realize they are very lucky.

Elizabeth did not want to leave her siblings in Africa. She was told beforehand that once she arrived and filled out the necessary paperwork, she could bring them over. This has not happened. Her sister is sixteen years old and her brothers are fifteen, thirteen, and nine years of age. The nine-year-old brother was the infant she carried in her arms in the desert. She believes her mother is alive, but does not know where she is. Her only explanation for her survival is that her faith led God to spare her. She describes the mind-set that happens when anyone is in that a desperate situation.

"When you are forced to live a desperate life, you know that you are on your own, and to survive, you have to have an intense desire to live. You must do whatever it takes and whatever you can to survive."

Elizabeth adds, "I like it here in the United States. Life is good, and I want this to be my home. However, I miss Africa, and if somehow there can ever be a lasting peace in Sudan, I might want to go back."

Priscilla Kuer

Our dream was to come to America, and we were filled with anticipation. Then on September 11, 2001—a day that at first seemed like any other—news began to spread throughout the camp. The Twin Towers in New York had been attacked by terrorists, and many American lives had been lost. Within a short time, there was weeping and praying throughout the camp. Within hours of that dreadful event America closed her borders.

Priscilla Kuer's Story

Twenty-four-year-old Priscilla Kuer is married to Joseph Deng, who is a Lost Boy. Typical of the people of the Dinka tribe, Priscilla is 6 feet 2 inches tall. She has a lovely face, and it is not unusual for people to stop her and ask her if she is a model. Priscilla and Joseph were born in the same village. Joseph was thirteen years old when their village was attacked. Priscilla was eight. Years later they met in the refugee camp in Kenya and fell in love. Joseph arrived in America in 2003. He has brothers who are still in the refugee camp in Kenya. Priscilla and their little girl, who is four years old, arrived in Dallas this year. Joseph and Priscilla both work for Central Market in Dallas. He is a cashier and she works in the bakery. They have a four-year-old daughter and a baby boy. Priscilla's story is as follows:

I lived in Wakulee, Sudan, which is in the Bor area. I had an eleven-year-old brother and two sisters, one ten years old, the other seven months. My sister and I were sleeping in the childrens' hut with all of the other children one night, when I was awoken by noises I had never heard before. The first sounds were explosions. They were bombs. Wherever the bombs hit, they made huge craters in what had once been a beautiful town.

The Arabs, who had surrounded our village beforehand, began racing through the streets in tanks and jeeps. Their faces were enraged, and they were screaming as they began shooting everyone in sight. Our houses were made out of grass, and the Arabs seemed to take great delight in setting them on fire.

The Arabs kidnapped the girls in our town who were fourteen and fifteen years old. If a young woman had a baby on her back, they would rip the baby away from the mother, throw it in a water vat where it would drown, or kill the baby and hang it in the trees. They shot all of the men and even the little boys.

I, along with other children, ran into the jungle. I couldn't understand why the Arabs were doing this. For a long time, I could hear people screaming and crying. It seemed to go on forever.

I decided I didn't know if there really was a God.

When it was silent, we came out of hiding and found other children along with a few adults. As children, we had no idea where we were going. We just followed the elders. For a few days we lived off of fruits that the older boys and girls found in the jungle. But then we came to the desert. Because it was so hot, the elders gathered us under any tree or shade we could find during the daytime. If we kept up with that group, we had a better chance to survive, but if any of us fell behind, we would die. We slept as much as we could. When the sun went down, we began walking. It was that first night that I heard a lion roar. I could tell he was very close and, next to gunfire and bombs, it was the most frightening sound I have ever heard in my life. We knew that if we slowed down or lay down to rest, the lion would get us. One night a lion grabbed my baby cousin. When we heard his screams, our hearts swelled with grief and froze with fear. The lion carried him away. It was horrible.

Later, we heard the older people talking about the lions. They said that the lions had eaten so many dead people, they had developed a taste for human flesh.

Lions seldom attack people until they taste carrion and realize what easy prey human beings can be. They can become dependent on human flesh for survival. Lions can move very fast and are usually bolder at night.

All of my life, I had never worried about water. Now there were days when there was no water and we had to drink our own urine. It was a desperate thing to have to do.

John Bul Dau, co-author of the book, God Grew Tired of Us, describes his suffering as a Lost Boy, when he nearly died from thirst in the desert in Sudan:

"My skin turned white," he says. "I cried, but there were no tears."

Thirst can lead to "hyperthermia," a condition where the body loses its ability to cool itself and thus overheats, resulting in the loss of body salts. The early stages of hyperthermia can cause cramps, headaches, and vomiting. Later more serious symptoms include delirium, unconsciousness, and finally, sudden death.

One day we passed a woman who was lying in the dirt. She was giving birth, but, except for a few people who stopped, everyone kept on walking. This poor woman did not have the comfort of being in her home surrounded by helpful women. Giving birth is a joyous event for the Dinka people. For her, it was not the happy occasion it was supposed to be. I never found out what happened to her or her baby. The memory of her lying in the dirt, in labor, lingered in my mind. Did she and her baby live or did they die? It was a scene that would come back to haunt me at a later time.

Most of us couldn't understand what was happening. We cried and cried. We were confused and tired. The elders had to urge us onwards to keep us walking. Sometimes they would trick us.

"There's a car up ahead with water and food. But we have to hurry or we will miss it," they said.

"OK," we said. Encouraged, we would walk a little faster. But where was the car? No matter how far we walked, the car was never there.

"Just a little further," the elders would urge. "We're almost there."

It became harder and harder to believe them.

Sometimes some of the smaller children would get mad and sit down and refuse to go on.

When that happened, if begging, pleading, and lying no longer worked, sometimes the older ones would lose their tempers and beat those children. Only when I was older did I realize they were resorting to desperate tactics to keep us alive. Those who were too little to understand, thought they were just being mean. Many of us decided we hated those bigger kids.

After fifteen days, we reached the refugee camp in Ethiopia. Finally we could feel safe because there were people to help us. Then I had a happy surprise. I found my brothers and my father. Even though the camp was dusty and barren, life suddenly seemed better. It was a happy reunion. I began to go to school and church. I decided I did believe in God once again.

It wasn't until we reached the camp that I found out the Arabs attacked us because we were Christians. I was told that the people who converted and became Muslims were branded. The name of Allah was burned onto their buttocks. When the Arabs attacked a village, the Muslims had to lower their pants to prove they were not Christians. It was only then that the Arabs would let them live.

In 1991, the camp in Ethiopia was attacked by the military. A change in government had brought in a new regime that was sympathetic to the cause of the Islamic Arabs. During that attack, just as in the attack on my village, people were running and screaming. Bombs were exploding in the camp, and as we all ran, soldiers were shooting at us. Many people died. Our only hope was to cross the Gilo River and escape back into Sudan. During that nightmarish scene, I remember seeing my father for the last time. He was a large, strong man, and my little brother and sister were clinging to his back as he swam towards the bank on the other side. Then I saw the bullets hit him. He and both of my siblings sank below the surface of the water, never to be seen again.

That scene is etched forever in my mind. To this day, no matter how hard I try, I cannot remember how I got across that river.

I am sure many of us were in shock as we traveled towards Kenya. By this time I was older and understood what was happening. Now I was one of the older children dragging the younger children along, and this time I was making false promises to keep them going. Yet, in some ways, this trip was a little easier because the Red Cross was there. They would race ahead of us in vans, leaving water, food, and blankets. But there was little they could do about the wild animals and the Arabs who were hunting us like animals. I remember feeling nothing, just a dogged determination to keep putting one foot in front of the other. In looking back, I realize now that we were all deeply traumatized.

Finally we arrived at a small village where the Red Cross had set up a station. Using a loudspeaker, every hour on the hour, they called out the names of refugees looking for their families. This was how I was reunited with my mother, sister, and baby brother. All we could do was hold each other and cry. I had thought they were all dead. Imagine thinking you would never see your mama again. Then suddenly she is there. It was one of the happiest moments of my life.

We reached the refugee camp in Kakuma, Kenya, in 1992. I went to school and learned English. But there were big problems. Even though the United Nations would bring in tanks with food and water, many times, mysteriously, the supplies would dwindle. Because fights would break out over water, when the UN workers arrived, they began spraying it in the air. Today there are wells. At first we were only given a liter of water a day. This was all of the water we had for drinking and cooking. On the third day we were given an extra liter for bathing. We lived in tents and the dust was terrible. Sometimes the wind was so strong it would knock our tents down. Yet, somehow life went on. I tried not to think about my sorrows and just do what I could to help my family and survive. It was after I became a camp counselor that I met Joseph. We discovered that we were from the same village. He was older than me, but I knew he was special. He had gone through the same experiences that I had endured, so we already had much in common. It wasn't long before we became very close.

With great happiness and celebration in our hearts, Joseph and I got married.

We talked constantly about our dreams to come to America, and just the thought of that wonderful country filled our minds with anticipation. Then on September 11, 2001—on a day that at first seemed like any other day—news began to spread throughout the camp. The Twin Towers in New York had been attacked by terrorists and many American lives had been lost. Within a short time, there was weeping and praying throughout the camp. Within hours of that dreadful event, America closed her borders.

Joseph and I had been scheduled to come to America in 2001. The UN workers tried to reassure us. "Don't despair," they said. "You have only been delayed. You will be allowed to go to America."

We didn't believe them. The very same people who had destroyed our lives were destroying them again. We were convinced we would be stuck in this terrible camp for the rest of our lives.

My sister was due to be interviewed by the United Nation's team, clearing her way to come to America. The interview was cancelled. Rumors spread like wildfire. One claimed that Osama bin Laden and his group, al-Qaeda, were hiding in the camp.

Hearing those rumors, the United Nations team became frightened and fled. When they left we felt like our hearts would break. There was much crying, sighing, and moaning throughout the camp in those days.

In 2003, when I was a few months pregnant, Joseph got his papers allowing him to go to America. I was sad to see him go, but happy that he would be able to go ahead to establish a home for our family.

Few people realize that the refugee camps in Kenya are very dangerous places. The security is stretched very thin. Armed groups of gangsters find out when the food and supplies are due to arrive and, at the critical time, make raids on the camp, after first determining which areas of the camp are the least secure. They rush in without giving any warning, shooting everyone in sight. There was a particularly vicious attack in July 2003 when I was pregnant with our little girl. When it happened, the hospital emptied immediately. It was common knowledge that the first thing these thugs do, once they get into the camp, is rush into the hospital searching for drugs. Without hesitation, they kill all of the staff and patients. Because of this, even though I was far advanced in my pregnancy, I knew I had to stay as far away from the hospital as possible.

As I ran for my life, the horrific memory of the woman giving birth in the dirt as I fled my village as a little girl, resurfaced in terrifying detail. Would I go into labor and have my baby on the ground? Would my baby and I die? Would there be anyone to help me if I went into labor?

I, along with several others, made our way to the United Nations compound where we barricaded ourselves for days. Finally, the president of Kenya sent government troops who battled the bandits and won. The camp, once again, was secure.

Priscilla's baby was born a month premature in the International Rescue Community Hospital. She weighed four pounds. Today she is a healthy, vibrant little girl who is tall for her age.

When Priscilla left Kenya, she was the only Lost Girl on the plane. Like her husband, she first flew to Chicago, then to Dallas.

"When I saw Chicago from the window of the plane, I felt like I was arriving in paradise," Priscilla says.

Priscilla's husband, Joseph, was waiting for her at the airport in Dallas. To Priscilla's delight, she already had a job. This was due to the fact that her husband had become a valued employee at Central Market. When he first began working, his job was to gather shopping carts in the parking lot. One day he found a bag in a cart that contained $3500. He took it to the office and turned it in. Within minutes a frantic woman called Central Market telling the people in the office she had lost her life savings. She was thrilled that the money had been found. The manager called Joseph into his office. "Joseph," he said. "We know you don't even have a car. We also know that a lot of people would never have turned that money in."

"I trust in God," Joseph had replied. "God is my money. I cannot make him angry by being dishonest."

Central Market immediately promoted Joseph and trained him as a cashier.

Joseph had no problem convincing Central Market to hire Priscilla when she arrived in Dallas. She works in the bakery.

Both Priscilla and Joseph have family members in the refugee camps in Kenya. Through the Red Cross they are able to stay in touch.

Joseph's parting words to me were: "You know, in many ways, because we went so long without our parents and suffered so much, we are like little children. You Americans are our mothers and fathers."

Like all of the Sudanese refugees I've met, Priscilla and Joseph suffer from terrible nightmares. But those bad dreams have begun to fade. They have nothing but praise for the American people, and their love for this country is deep. They are extremely patriotic.

Chapter Eleven

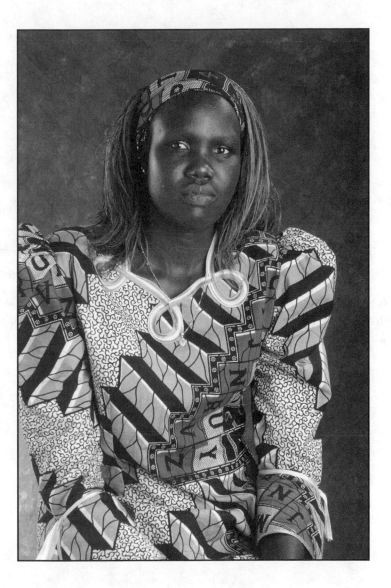

Rebecca Kuer

We shared everything, so we were delighted when we were given a large bag of clothing. But, when we divided it, there was not enough to go around. If you were given a shirt or blouse, you had to go bottomless. Or if you got a pair of pants or a skirt, you didn't have a top. It might have been funny, if it wasn't so sad.

Rebecca Kuer's Story

Rebecca Kuer, the mother of a little boy, is Priscilla Deng's sister. The second born of two brothers and three sisters, she was five years old when the Arabs attacked her village. She is engaged to a Lost Boy. Her mother Deborah, who lives with her, does not speak any English. They do not have a car, and whenever Rebecca can find temporary work in factories, she rides the bus. Her story is as follows:

The attack happened early in the morning. We woke up to the sound of guns. "The Arabs are coming," my mother said as she grabbed my baby sister.

I, along with my sister Priscilla and two of my brothers, ran into the forest where Mother hid us.

My mother then ran in a different direction holding the baby. She knew that if the baby cried it would lead the Arabs to her.

Because she put herself at great risk by saving the baby, she had already decided that if they did find her, at least the rest of us might survive.

I remember how we were all quiet as mice, watching from our hiding place in the trees, as the Arabs moved through the bush searching for us.

I was very confused. I couldn't understand why the Arabs wanted to kill us.

When we came out of hiding and began walking, Momma carried the little ones, usually two at a time, holding one child in the front and carrying the other on her back.

We suffered terribly in the desert. The sun was relentless. There were scorpions, snakes, wild animals, and dangerous men who, time and time again, attacked us on the way.

It was during this time that I saw many dead bodies and people dying on the side of the road. They were killed by soldiers or died from heat, exhaustion, or thirst. We were so desperate, we drank our own urine. We didn't have shoes or clothes so our feet hurt, and at night, when the desert gets cold, we would shiver and cry. We were filthy.

When we got terribly thirsty, the glands in our necks swelled, making our throats very sore. Then every word we uttered caused our throats to hurt. When we did find water, the temptation was to drink it very fast, but some who did this died.

Mother kept urging us on. We cried and cried every day. We were so confused. What happened to our nice village or our lives where we were never hungry? In those good days we played until we got tired, then some big person would take us carefully to the sleeping hut and lay us down on our nice, soft mats. There was always laughter and singing. Now it was all gone. Sometimes I couldn't help but wonder if this was just not a bad dream. Maybe, if we could just go home, it would be as it was before. "But no," mother said. "That life was over, and to stay alive we had to keep walking."

Only when I was grown did I understand the fear my mother

lived with day after day. She had to live with the reality that all of us could die. Is there anything more painful than a mother losing her children? Often there was an expression of blankness on my mother's face and she no longer sang.

Sometimes we got too tired and weak. Then we would sit down and refuse to go on. Patiently she would sit down with us and talk to us quietly. She told us there was food and water just up ahead. We never seemed to reach it, but we kept hoping she was right.

Meanwhile, we had to keep running. The Arabs would fly overhead in helicopters, and, when they spotted us, soldiers would lean out of the doors, dropping bombs and shooting at us with machine guns. We lived in constant fear.

One month later, we finally arrived at the refugee camp in Ethiopia. We were reunited with our father and thought that we were safe, but even in the camp there were problems. Our parents were the only ones who could go to the river to get water because of the crocodiles. My father immediately built us a house. At first it was mud with brush. Later when the United Nations arrived, they gave us plastic tarps which we draped in a tree and covered with leaves, hoping to keep cool. It was still very hot, but we settled in. The peace did not last.

Very early one morning, we woke up to those dreaded but familiar sounds: a shrill whistle, followed by a moment of silence, then a huge noise as the bombs fell. Next came the screaming of madmen, armed with guns, as they raced into the camp, killing people savagely. All of them had such expressions of glee and hatred on their faces, as they lit the huts on fire and killed and killed again.

We ran to the river. A man on the other side was lowering a rope for people to hang onto as he lifted them up to the bank. He was amazingly strong.

It was during this horrible time that my father, with my little brother and sister clinging to his back, was shot as he tried to swim across the water. They all died.

Even when we reached the other side we were not safe. The Arabs continued to bomb and shoot us. In all of the confusion, my sister and I became separated from our mother. I truly did not know if I would live.

"Why do they enjoy killing us so much?" I asked someone.

"It's because they think they are doing Allah's will," was the answer.

I was glad Allah was not my god. The Christian God is kind. He never wanted us to kill another person. He is a God of love and forgiveness.

Again, we found ourselves in a group of displaced people. When older people saw we were alone, they took care of us. This time we weren't forced to starve because the United Nations people came with a limited amount of water, food, and clothing.

We shared everything, so we were delighted when we were given a large bag of clothing. But, when we divided it, there was not enough to go around. If you were given a shirt or blouse, you had to go bottomless. Or if you got a pair of pants or a skirt, you didn't have a top. It might have been funny, if it wasn't so sad.

We finally reached Kapeota, and this is where we found our mother. She hugged us over and over, and later that night, for the first time since our village had been raided, she began to sing. Her voice was so beautiful it comforted us all.

Then, like a recurring nightmare, Kapeota was bombed and we had to run again. Finally we reached Kakuma. Life was hard because there was often not enough food or water. You only got a meal once a day. There was never enough medicine. When sickness came, people died. This would be my home for the next ten years.

In Kakuma, the government did provide security. When the bad people in the camp attacked, the government sent in their soldiers to restore order.

We talked to the missionaries, and many times they wrote down our stories. Sometimes the process was very slow, but finally in 2001 I was interviewed. I was afraid to leave because I feared the unknown. Our friends and families urged us to go to other countries so we could make money and help them get out of the camp.

Then the attack on the United States happened on September 11.

"God, what happened?" I prayed. Everyone was very sad. We all prayed, everyday. Then the rumor spread that al-Qaeda and the Taliban were hiding in the camp. Those were fearful days. We were suspicious of every new face. Were there terrorists hiding among us?

In Sudan, even today, people pray everyday because there is such terrible suffering. They pray in groups in the morning, again at noon, and then in the evening. On Sundays everyone goes to church.

Finally, the big day came and I found myself on the airplane headed out of Africa. Sitting by the door, I was afraid to look out of the window. When our plane approached London, I finally got up the courage. When I looked out the window and saw all of the beautiful lights, I was suddenly very happy.

It seems as if, at every turn, there were people to help us on our way. A Lost Boy met us at the plane in Chicago. He told us he had waited for four hours.

When we arrived at DFW on February 7, 2006, people from an agency took us to our new homes.

I was used to eating only rice, so it took me some time to get used to the food.

The memories that haunt me to this day are the shootings and the image of my father and my siblings, drowning with so many others.

My country has paid a terrible price for the evil that has been done. The only way I will ever go back is when we no longer hear the sound of guns. Everyday, when I wake up I think about those prayers in the camp. I know that God answers prayers and someday He will restore Africa to the paradise it once was.

Chapter Twelve

Mama Deborah Bol

Like the hyenas, we became scavengers. When we found the carcass of a dead animal, we would cook and eat it. First, we would create a fire by boring a hole into a piece of wood. Then, we would position a stick in that hole and spin it with the palms of our hands, until the friction started a small flame. We would dig a hole and cook the meat. This had to be done in the daytime. We could not light fires at night because the Arabs would see the flames.

Mama Deborah Bol's Story

Deborah, the mother of Priscilla and Rebecca, speaks no English. She is a quiet, unassuming woman. Few people realize that she survived the horrors of civil war in Sudan by carrying her own children, along with her sister's children, to safety. Today she takes English classes on Saturdays, walks to the bus, and lives a quiet life. Her story is as follows:

We had to keep running from place to place. Whenever we found a tree, we would hide, hoping the Arabs couldn't see us, but always we were forced to run again.

There were many dangers. Trees meant shade and firewood, but often there were poisonous snakes in those trees. Many people died after being bitten by those snakes. Then there were the wild beasts, the lions and the hyenas. Like animals, we were hunted, not only by the beasts of the jungle but by the Arabs as well.

Whenever we heard the sound of helicopters overhead, we would hide the best we could. They would swoop down close to the ground, and then soldiers, leaning out of the doors, would throw bombs and shoot as many of us as possible. The killing seemed to go on and on. All we could do was keep running and hoping we would not be killed.

"God, if you don't save me, please save my children," I prayed, day after day.

Like the hyenas, we too became scavengers. When we found the carcass of a dead animal, we would cook and eat it. First, we would create a fire by boring a hole into a piece of wood. Then, we would position a stick in that hole and spin it with the palms of our hands, until the friction started a small flame. We would dig a hole and cook the meat. This had to be done in the daytime. We could not light fires at night because the Arabs would see the flames.

Often we were desperate from hunger and thirst. We ate the leaves and bark off of trees. Sometimes the leaves were very bitter and, occasionally, even poisonous. We saw people die from eating leaves.

We had to coax the children, and often my husband and I kept them going by telling them lies. "There's food and water just up ahead," we would say. "Come on, it's just a little further. You can do it."

My husband complimented the children, telling them how strong they were. They tried to please him, but compliments and lies didn't always work.

After hours of walking they would begin to cry. They were confused and angry and sometimes would sit down and refuse to budge. Then, I would sit down and talk to them. My heart still hurts when I think about their suffering. None of them had shoes or clothing. Their feet were blistered and sore. Often I felt helpless, but I knew we had to keep them going, at any cost.

Finally we arrived at the camp in Ethiopia. The United

Nations hadn't arrived yet, so my husband built our hut from scratch. Later, when the United Nations did come, they gave us flour and a plastic tarp. We covered it with grass, trying to insulate it, hoping we could stay cooler in the daytime and warmer at night. It was flimsy shelter, but it was all we had.

We were in the camp for almost five years when, early one morning, I awoke to hear the dreaded sounds of bombs and guns. The camp was under attack.

I grabbed three of the children and ran to the river. My husband ran with the other two. As I put Rebecca and Priscilla in a boat, I looked back to see a scene that will forever break my heart.

My little girl, who was the two-month-old baby I had saved when I ran from the Arabs, along with her brother, were clinging to their father's back. As he began to swim across the river, suddenly out of nowhere, a bullet found its mark. Shot in the head, he sank beneath the surface of the water. I could only watch helplessly as the children drowned in a river that was now red with blood. First my heart broke, then a grey fog enveloped my mind. Had I gone through all of this to save my children, only to see them die one by one? I no longer had a husband to help me through life's trials.

Again we were outcasts. I had gathered as many supplies as I could carry, and this time, there were people from the United Nations who helped us. We ended up in the camp in Kenya and it was there that my daughters went to school. I am proud of the women they have become, and today I no longer live in fear. I am safe, living in America with my daughter Rebecca. But at night, the dreams come, and they are always the same. In vivid detail, I see my husband swimming strongly across a vast river with my daughter and son on his back. Then, suddenly I see blood exploding from his head. I cry as he sinks, taking my children to a watery grave.

It's bad being a widow, but no mother should ever lose her children. It's a heartbreak that can never be healed.

Chapter Thirteen

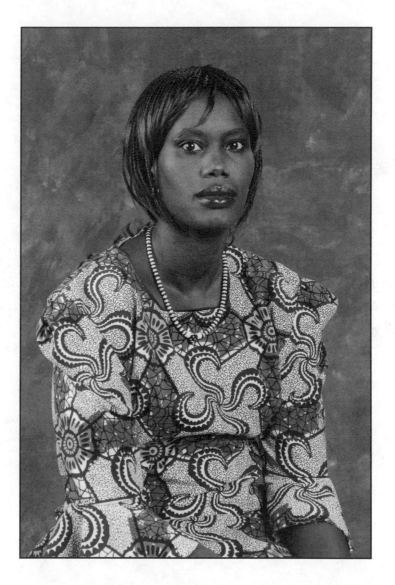

Elisabeth Akuen

I wore an old burlap sack, and I was barefoot. But that was probably for the best, because if you were wearing good clothes it could be the death of you. Someone who decided they liked those clothes could kill you for them.

Elizabeth Akuen's Story

Elizabeth Akuen came to Dallas in February of 2006. Her cousin translated for her because her English is still very limited. Elizabeth has three children. Her daughter Kahmis is five years old, her son Nhial is seven years old, and her other daughter, Abuk, is an infant. Their father, Abraham Jok, who works for Presbyterian Hospital, is a Lost Boy.

Upon my arrival, Elizabeth's children rushed to meet me. The little girl announced she was in kindergarten, and the little boy proudly proclaimed he was in the first grade. When they saw my notebook, they each politely requested a piece of paper, before their mother sternly lectured them in Dinka, sending them into the other room.

The only surviving member from Elizabeth's immediate family is her mother who lives in southern Sudan. Elizabeth's story is as follows:

I was born in a village in southern Sudan. The Arabs attacked my village in 1991. It happened late at night. I was only ten years old at the time. First came the horrifying sound of the bombs. Then the soldiers poured into the village in their jeeps and trucks. I had been asleep in the childrens' hut when I was awakened by the noise and confusion.

I ran outside, and to my amazement the whole village seemed

to be on fire. Stunned, I ran to my house. Then, for one brief moment, all of the screaming and noise seemed to fade into silence as I stared in disbelief at my father's body lying on the ground. Where was the large, happy man that we all adored? This couldn't be him. His body, oozing blood from various places, looked awkward sprawled in the dirt. My Poppa, my protector, and the strongest and most handsome man in the world, was dead. The Arabs had shot him.

The next thing I knew I was running. The fear made me run so fast, it seemed as if my feet had wings, as I ran into the bush. I didn't even knowing where I was going, but I knew if the Arabs found me, they would kill me. My whole body shook with sorrow as I tried to smother my crying. I had to choke back the tears because I knew it was important to be quiet.

Hours later, I heard voices and crying as other children started coming out of hiding. Now there was no village to go home to. The Arabs had not only burned our entire village, they had killed the livestock, thrown the dead bodies into the wells, and burned all of our crops. I couldn't grasp the fact that my family was gone. Thinking of my mother, I sobbed, believing the Arabs had killed her.

Before long I found myself part of a large group of people. Most of them, like me, were children. We were all bewildered and confused. "Why do they hate us?" I asked someone.

"It's because we're Christians and refused to convert," was the answer.

I couldn't understand why someone would want to kill us because of our religion. We were just people who wanted to take care of our livestock and live our lives in our village. It was beyond understanding. The world, as I knew it, was gone.

Most of us didn't know where we were going or what we were going to do. Some decided it was better to walk during the day and others chose to walk at night.

We soon found out that if you walked during the day the Arabs would spot you in their airplanes and drop their bombs. When we heard a plane, we would drop into the nearest ditch and cover our heads. We could only pray the bombs would not land on us. The bombs contained razor blades and pieces of lead, and if they hit you they would cut you to pieces.

Then there were the Arabs who hid in the bushes, with their guns. When they saw you, without a sound, they would shoot you. I saw many people killed as we walked. Along the way there were many dead bodies. I could not help but wonder. Would I die on the side of the road like so many others?

If you walked during the night, your fear turned to the animals that were predators. The lions and hyenas began feeding on the bodies, and each day they became bolder.

All I owned in the world was what I wore. It was an old sack that once had been full of maize. But that probably was for the best, because if you were wearing good clothes it could be the death of you. Someone who decided they liked those clothes could kill you for them.

I was barefoot, so it wasn't long before my feet began to cause me great suffering. Because I couldn't see where I was going at night, I stepped on thorns. Thorns are very long and sharp in

Africa. My feet began to bleed and swell. They hurt so badly I was forced to walk on the back of my heels. Hobbling along, I did my best to keep up with the others. I knew I couldn't stop walking. If I did I would die like so many people who had died along the way.

Numbness took over my mind and each day, as I lurched along, I only hoped God would let me live another day. Walking, thirst, hunger, these things became all that I could think about. I chewed grass and even ate leaves. Many people died because of starvation and dehydration.

Weak and thin, we finally arrived at Loki where we found help. It was 1990, and it was a miracle that we had survived. We would stay there until we arrived at the refugee camp Kakuma in 1992.

The town of Lokichoggio (referred to as Loki) is close to the border of Sudan and serves as the gateway between southern Sudan and Kenya. Many United Nations and World Food Program planes crowd the runway. Several agencies use the town as a staging post for aid going into Sudan and Kakuma. Every day people arrive and stay briefly before they are taken to the refugee camp in Kakuma.

Life in Kakuma is very hard. There is only one meal a day. If you eat it in the morning, you go to bed hungry at night. If you eat at night, you are hungry in the morning. That meal is almost always maize, which is made into porridge, and sometimes, on good days, there are lentils. The medical help is very hard to get, so you can only pray that you do not get ill. But at least the government in Kenya tries to protect the camp.

I came to America in February of 2006. We first flew to London, then Chicago, then on to Dallas.

My world, which had turned upside down when the Arabs attacked our village, suddenly spun around, and this time, I landed on my feet. I found myself in a land that seemed like magic. The good lifestyle that people enjoy is something I could not have imagined in my wildest dreams. I am amazed at how well people have treated us. They brought us clothing, furnishings, and food. They even take us to the stores. Sometimes I feel overwhelmed. There are things that confuse me, and I admit, I get nervous in traffic.

I still have nightmares, and I often find myself thinking about Africa and how the war affected me along with so many other people. When people ask me what was the very worst thing during those times, I tell them it was the destruction of the family. There are no family reunions, and our history is lost. It is a big heartbreak.

For years I worried about my mother. I was afraid that she died. But finally I found her. She now lives in the southern part of Sudan. My hope is to bring her to America. Mothers are important in our culture. They help us take care of our children. I am all she has left, and I want her to be with me at the end of her days.

For myself, the thing I want more than anything in the world is an education. It concerns me that it does not seem possible at this time. But America is wonderful, and often the impossible becomes possible in a surprising way. I thank God everyday that

He carried me through the desert and brought me to this land that is full of kind-hearted people.

Elizabeth speaks very little English, so her cousin, who is a Lost Boy, acted as our interpreter. Like every home I visited, her home was immaculate. Again, I left the interview in awe. I find the resilience and optimism of these people truly amazing.

Chapter Fourteen

Mary Pediet

It was while running from Kayi that we met a group of rebel soldiers on the road as we were fleeing. They had come to help the villagers. My son, who was 25 years old, had been drafted in 1990. It was 1992, and he was among those soldiers we met on the road. We had just a few minutes together before he had to rejoin his unit and move on. I didn't realize then I would never see him again. Within days, he would be killed by the Arabs.

Mary Pediet's Story

Mary is a care-worn Sudanese woman of fifty-seven years. She does not speak English, so with the help of her daughter and sons, I was able to piece this story together. Despite her English limitations, she has just gotten a minimum-wage job. Even though three of her sons and one daughter are here, she is distraught, for good reason. Originally, she lived in a village in the Duk area of Sudan. She had six children. Like so many others, when she heard the sound of gunfire, she fled. Her story is as follows:

The attack happened at night. We were awakened by terrible noise. My husband and I grabbed everything we could and ran outside. When I saw my little sister, I picked her up and ran.

The Arabs set the entire village on fire. We hid in the trees. Then the ground forces moved in. One of my sons was killed in that attack.

Two of my brothers headed for Ethiopia. Taking the smaller children, my husband and I walked to Kayi, Sudan. But we weren't able to stay for a single day, because the Arabs attacked there also.

It was while running from Kayi that we met a group of rebel soldiers on the road as we were fleeing. They had come to help the villagers. My son, who was 25 years old, had been drafted in 1990. It was 1992, and he was among those soldiers we met on the road.

We had just a few minutes together before he had to rejoin his unit and move on. I didn't realize then I would never see him again because, a short time later, he was killed by the Arabs.

We suffered terribly. No shoes, no clothes, no water, and no food. We resorted to eating leaves and anything else we could get our hands on. We saw a lot of dead bodies, and we were forced to sleep on the ground. It was burning hot during the day and cold at night. There were also wild animals.

When you are in these trying times, to survive, you learn to live minute to minute. This is how your time goes by. When you reach that next minute, you can only wait to see what will happen next. I had already decided that even if I died, I wanted my children to live. They are the future.

The Arabs attacked again and again. Yet, somehow, some of us survived.

After a year, we arrived in Kenya, where we joined a huge group of refugees. Every hour on the hour, the government announced new arrivals who were coming into the camp. We kept checking, and to our delight, we were reunited with my sisters.

We were in the refugee camp for five long years. Many times we were hungry. You stood in line at specific times waiting for water. If you were at the end of the line and the water ran out you were out of luck. You had just enough water for drinking.

As for the food, it was the same thing. There were fifteen kilos per person for the month. You ate once a day. There is never enough. Sometimes the food is delayed for up to fifteen days.

The Turkana, local people who live in that area, would sometimes attack the people in the camp. Each month I would see five or ten people die.

The medical help is limited. If you get sick, you either get well on your own or you will probably die. There is not enough security.

When I arrived in Dallas, I was amazed at the prosperity of this city. My children here are flourishing, but I am torn and do not sleep at night. My daughter Arok, is still in the refugee camp in Kenya. She is in her thirties and has five children. Her husband, who was bitten by a crocodile when he fled from his village, was never able to get the proper medical treatment. The wound festered until the flesh began falling away from the bone. He died recently. I was told he was talking, up to the moment of his death.

The worst thing in my life was losing my two sons, along with family members.

Now my daughter is a widow. How can she feed her children? I worry about them everyday. Maybe I should go back to be with her. I am in torment.

Mary's sons hold part-time jobs and go to school. Her daughter, Nynwar, is married to a Lost Boy and is pregnant. Whatever extra money the family can scrape together they send to Arok, but, with five children, it is never enough. This is why, even though she doesn't have transportation and cannot speak English, Mary has somehow managed to get a job so she can help her daughter in the camp.

Mary's sons report that an American couple, they call Jim and Cathy, has become their American family. They spend the holidays with them, have helped them adjust to living in Dallas, and have taken them to church and school.

Typical of the Sudanese people I have met, Mary has nothing but praise for America and its people, and, like the others I've interviewed, she has a deep well of spiritual faith. Her final word before I left:

"Thank you, America. Thank you, God."

Chapter Fifteen

Nyanwuor

Suddenly, all of the cows were gone. The Arabs had slaughtered them. There was no milk. For the Sudanese, this was a disaster.

We were all accustomed to drinking milk, and many of our meals were cooked in milk. Just the thought of milk no longer being available traumatized some people so badly; they just gave up and died.

Nyanwuor's Story

Nyanwuor, Mary's daughter, is married to a Lost Boy. Tall and slender, she is beautiful. She is pregnant with her first child and the baby is due in March. Her brother, Dwok, was the first to migrate to the United States. After he arrived, he received help from Catholic Charities. Because she was a young child at the time, Nyanwuor's memories of Sudan are dim. Unfortunately, she had some bad experiences after she arrived in Dallas. Her story is as follows:

I remember my brother warning us that the military was coming, and I remember hiding during the daytime. We could only come out at night. If we ate at night, we had to cook inside because the Arabs would see the fires and find us.

I also remember the bombing. When the bombs fell, we had to lie on the ground.

It's funny what remains in a child's mind, because one of my most vivid memories is about milk.

Suddenly, all of the cows were gone. The Arabs had slaughtered them. Because of this, there was no milk. For the Sudanese, this was a disaster.

We were all accustomed to drinking milk, and many of our meals were cooked in milk. Just the thought of milk no longer being available traumatized some people so badly, they just gave up and died.

My sister warned me not to think about milk and even went so far as to forbid me to even say the word. I began to play a game. When I poured water over my gruel, I pretended it was milk.

I remember the time when there was no food and water. Those were hard days. I remember crying and walking. A lot of us cried, but our parents made us keep going.

Then, I remember being reunited with my mother in the refugee camp. I thought she was dead, and she thought we were dead, so when we saw each other, we all cried and cried.

My brother Dwok was the first to come to America. My mother and I, along with two more of my brothers, were finally able to come. We thought everyone else would come later.

I was seventeen years old when I first came to Dallas. It was an amazing new world. It was like something out of a book or science fiction. I was fascinated by all of the tall buildings. This is a totally different environment from what we knew in Africa.

Then there were the cars, in every size, shape, and color. In the camp, we would see a car maybe once a week, or, when things were really busy, once a day. I had never seen so many cars in my life, and they were all moving at a great speed. It was unnerving, to say the least. Now I ride in a car all over town and just like Americans everywhere, I don't give it a second thought.

I was seventeen when I enrolled in Bryan Adams High School, then later transferred to Hillcrest High School. I couldn't understand English, but it soon became apparent that because I am so dark, the black kids were making fun of my skin. When the teacher wasn't looking they would shove me around and laugh. When I went to the teacher she did not give me any support. One day, it became too much. I went home early and never went back. For the first time in my life, I began to regret my color. To this day, African-Americans make comments about the color of my skin. I can't understand why they do this. It's hard when people stare.

My mother is always worried about my sister in Kenya. I feel so bad about her, and I shudder when I think how her husband died. To survive a crocodile bite is a miracle in itself. But then, not to be able to get medical treatment is a tragedy. The fact that my sister is a widow with five children is a great hardship. Everyone in her husband's family is dead, so she has no one. My brothers and I see the toll this is taking on our mother. She has seen too much sorrow and known too much grief. If we could somehow manage to get my sister and her children here, then my mother would be content.

I came to America to have freedom and a good life. This is a wonderful country. I am shocked when people make excuses not to do something because of their race. I know that in this country, one can do anything if he or she works hard enough. This is the land of opportunity, and my greatest wish is that someday I can be in a position to help other people.

Chapter Sixteen

Mary Malual

We hid in the reeds. After it was quiet, I crept back to the house. Everyone was gone.

Alone and lost, I began to cry as I struggled to keep up with a group of people I did not know. I walked for almost two days, wondering where my family had gone?

At the end of the second day a big man walked back and took me by the hand. He began yelling, "This little girl Mary has lost her family. Does anyone know where they are? God granted my wish. Because of this kind man, they found me.

Mary Malual's Story

Mary Malual is 23 years old. Married to Akec Ajak (a Lost Boy), she has a ten month-old baby boy. She was born in the southern area of Sudan in the city of Abei. She had three brothers and two sisters. Born in 1984, she was only three years old when the Arabs attacked her village and killed her father. She attends culinary school. Her story is as follows:

My memories are dim about the first attack. My father was killed and my family was scattered. My older sister Elizabeth, who was seven at the time, took care of me. I remember walking and being hungry, frightened, and thirsty. It took two and one half years for us to get to the refugee camp in Ethiopia where we were united with the rest of our family. I am amazed that we survived.

In 1991, I was almost eight years old when the government in Ethiopia was overthrown and the new government attacked the camp. First came the bombs, then the soldiers with guns. I saw my cousin killed right before my eyes.

I was lucky because my uncle was a commander in the SPLA who also worked in security. He grabbed my sister Elizabeth and me as he raced towards the river. I remember clinging to his back as he carried us across. I saw many people die that day. Bombs; gunfire; screaming; crocodiles lunging, clamping their terrible jaws around helpless people in the water; and the King Cobra snake, striking people as they ran—these images surpassed the worst scenes in the most horrific of nightmares. Unfortunately for us, there were no actors and props. We were real people, and the horror was real.

My uncle saved our lives that day. It was too late for my cousin, however. He had been killed within minutes of the Arabs attacking the camp.

We finally reached Fascila. I remember the adults sitting with worried expressions on their faces as they prayed fervently for my uncle's little three-year-old girl. She had been sick for some time. She died soon after we arrived, and we were very sad.

The elders sent me, along with my sister, to the river to fetch water. While we were there, the soldiers attacked again. Out of nowhere came the airplanes, dropping their bombs, followed by the bullets, fires, and screams that seemed to go on forever. Even though we were children, we now knew what these noises meant.

We hid in the reeds. Finally I stood up. Where was my sister? When it was quiet, I crept back to the house. Everyone was gone. Alone, I began to cry as I struggled to keep up with a group of people I did not know. I walked for almost two days, wondering where my family had gone. At the end of the second day, a big man walked back through the crowd and took my hand.

He began yelling, "This little girl Mary has lost her family. Does anyone know where they are?" God granted me my wish. Because of this kind man, they found me.

We didn't have clothes or shoes. There was no water or food. We lived with the constant threat of soldiers, wild animals, snakes, and poisonous spiders.

After one and a half months, we arrived in Kapota.

In June 1992, the government attacked again. Many of the people ran into the church when the bombs fell. They were burned alive.

Again God spared us, because we escaped. I ended up in the refugee camp in Kenya where I lived for eleven years with the uncle who had rescued me. I met my husband in the refugee camp. I came to America in 2004, and we got married soon after I arrived.

My sister's husband, who was in the rebel army, was killed in 2000, leaving her with three children. I remember how well she took care of me. Now I do my best to try and take care of her. I worry because she is sick, and I send money whenever I can.

Mary believes the Sudanese people were persecuted because they refused to convert. She also believes that many of the people in Africa who have converted did so because of force.

When you convert for fear of your life, because you are at the wrong end of a gun, is this a true conversion?

Unlike most of the Lost Girls, Mary was able to go back and visit her family in Africa recently before her child was born.

I miss Africa with all of my heart and I miss my family. As the time came close for me to leave, I thought about staying. But my husband is here, and my sister said, "You have to return. It's only you who can help us now."

My wish is that I can someday become educated and have a career so I can help my family. I worry about them all of the time. If the war continues, I hope I can bring them here.

Author's Note:

I know there are probably more Lost Girls in Dallas, but I am sure, if I could find them, their stories would be sadly familiar. They've all endured heartbreak and horrible suffering, but they each possess an indomitable spirit and a strong will to survive. Their stories will hopefully act as a wake-up call to Americans. As one Lost Boy said, "America is the last great place." I can only hope the Lost Girls' stories can open our eyes.

Chapter Seventeen

The Journey

Before I met the Lost Girls, I knew there were severe problems in Africa. Like everyone, I've become accustomed to seeing scenes of war played out on the television screen. I've been bewildered by the indifference shown by leaders of state and saddened by the heartbreaking images of starving children. I've been baffled by the endless rhetoric and appalled by the heads of state in Africa who smile and say it's all an exaggeration. Invariably, those same interviews are followed by horrific images of suffering. The endless stream of information goes on, but the conclusion is always the same. Innocent children, along with their families, continue to suffer and die. A perfect example of this is what has occurred in Sudan and is now occurring in Darfur.

Years ago, the United Nations approved a motion that if and when genocide occurred, a peace-keeping military presence would be sent into the afflicted area. Yet, even as evidence is brought to us by mainstream news concerning the calamity in Africa, nothing is done.

Like many people, my solution was to shake my head in disbelief, make a few comments and then move on with my life, living in a state of denial. In meeting and talking to the Lost Girls and their husbands (most of them Lost Boys), my eyes have been opened.

Emotionally and mentally, as I've written each story, I've seen the horrific images in my mind of the dreaded Janjaweed. I've tried to imagine the fear of those lost children as they wearily put one foot in front of the other, as they moved through a barren and ruined landscape planted with bombs. I've tried to understand each child's despair and tried to imagine what it would be like to be hungry to the point of starvation. I've tried to relate to the torture one experiences from extreme thirst, when the tongue becomes swollen, lips split, and the skin becomes parched beyond endurance.

These lost children lived with the constant threat of danger, the lack of security, and the emotional burdens of sorrow and fear.

Never did I realize that in writing this book I would find myself embarking on a journey where I would emerge on the other side changed. I feel a connection to the people of Africa, and I am convinced that we cannot afford to stand by helplessly as this injustice continues. I believe that we as Americans can no longer be complacent.

Only now have I fully begun to comprehend the devastation refugees must feel when they lose their loved ones, their country, their history, and their identity.

Even though the Lost Girls of Sudan and many refugees from all over the world have seen the very worst in mankind, they have managed to keep their faith in God.

Psychiatrists across the nation agree that they are the most traumatized people in the world. Yet, the Lost Girls I have met, have managed to pick up the pieces and rebuild their lives. They, more than most of us, appreciate what this country represents.

As one Lost Boy told me, "America is the last great place."

I have come to understand that the Lost Girls and Lost Boys do not want to be viewed as victims. They are descended from a long line of proud people. Many of them would like to see their native country restored. They would like to see their remaining relatives, who are languishing in the refugee camps, released into their care. Only time will tell, if they will ever see the perpetrators who destroyed their land, their people, and their history brought to justice.

Each Lost Girl and Lost Boy that I have met is highly intelligent. They are hard workers, are exceedingly loyal, and have a deep sense of integrity. They have put their faith in the United States. I am convinced that their being here is of great benefit to our country.

The Lost Girls and Lost Boys represent a deep well of faith and resilience. Their heartbreaking journey through the wilderness has provided us with examples of courage and tenacity. I have come to believe that, no matter what, the human spirit cannot be quenched. Mankind will survive. I owe all of the Lost Girls, who were willing to open their hearts and share their painful, heartbreaking memories with me, a debt of gratitude. They have not only inspired me, they have deepened my faith.

About the Author

Beverly Parkhurst Moss fell headlong into publishing in 1971 by accident. The sole supporter of a handicapped husband and three children, she wanted to earn some extra money for Christmas, so she published her first tabloid *The Intowner*, which was an insert in the *Dallas Times Herald*. It became a popular monthly insert that was eventually carried by the *Dallas Morning News* from 1978 until 1986. Her next magazine, *Discoveries Old and New*, was carried in the *Dallas Morning News* until 2001, when she lost her husband and oldest son within a twelve-day period. She currently publishes *Lifestyle Solutions*, a target-marketed, bi-monthly publication.

In the late '70s, Beverly co-authored the book *Beating Men at Their Own Game* (a self help book for women in sales). The book was originally published by Wiley and Sons and later released in paperback by Simon and Schuster, and received good national reviews.

In the '80s, Beverly self-published a collection of her *Sincerely* columns. In 2004 and 2005, she wrote two biographies—one for restaurant guru Johnny Walker, and the other for World War II veteran and owner of Centennial Liquor Jim Vandeveer.

Her inspiration for the book *Dark Exodus* came in May of 2007 after attending a small evening function held by a women's group, The Steel Magnolias, at the Fellowship Bible Church in Dallas. During that event, she found out, to her amazement, that there are not only Lost Boys of Sudan in Dallas, there are also Lost Girls.

"Why didn't I know about this?" she wondered. A few days later, as she was getting ready for work, the concept for the book along with the cover design fell into her mind instantly.

When she met with these Lost Girls the following weekend, they not only agreed to be interviewed, they said, "Finally, we will be heard."

The book, *Dark Exodus*, contains the stories of sixteen amazing women, some who were as young as four years old when their villages were burned, and they were forced to flee into the forests and deserts of Sudan, where some of them walked for hundreds of miles before they found their way into refugee camps. They dealt with lions, hyenas, government soldiers, and hostile tribesmen along the way. They survived hunger, dehydration, and horrendous suffering along with the loss of friends and family.

"These women are true heroines," Beverly Parkhurst Moss says.

Fifty percent of the proceeds from the sale of the book, *Dark Exodus*, will go to the Lost Girls to help them with their educations, career training, and the rescue of relatives who are still languishing in refugee camps.